You Don't Know Anything…!

You Don't Know Anything a manuel For Parenting Teenagers

MF

You Don't Know Anything...!

A Manual for Parenting Your Teenagers

Nadir Baksh, Psy.D.
and Laurie Murphy, Ph.D.

HOHM PRESS
Prescott, Arizona

Cover design, layout and interior design: Zachary Parker, Kadak Graphics, Prescott, AZ (www.kadakgraphics.com).

Library of Congress Cataloging-in-Publication Data

Baksh, Nadir.
 You Don't Know Anything...! : a manual for parenting your teenagers / Nadir Baksh and Laurie Murphy.
      p. cm.
 Includes index.
 ISBN 978-1-890772-82-6 (trade pbk. : alk. paper)
 1. Parent and teenager. 2. Teenagers--Family relationships. 3. Teenagers--Psychology. 4. Parenting. I. Murphy, Laurie. II. Title.
 HQ799.15.B35 2008
 649'.125--dc22

                              2008011318

HOHM PRESS
P.O. Box 2501
Prescott, AZ 86302
800-381-2700
http://www.hohmpress.com

This book was printed in the U.S.A. on recycled, acid-free paper using soy ink.

This book is dedicated to parents everywhere whose love endures despite the adversity and anguish of the teenage years.

Acknowledgements

There are so many people who have helped to shape us and had such enormous impact on the direction our lives have taken. Some of these individuals have since passed away, and although they are no longer physically present, their spirit motivates us to work harder, love deeper and never settle for second best. We miss them dearly. There are those who continue to share their lives with us, especially our parents and children, who have always supported our dreams, loving us despite our shortcomings, or because of them. We love them dearly.

There are those who continue to share their lives with us, especially our parents and children, who have always supported our dreams, loving us despite our shortcomings, or because of them. We love them dearly.

Then there are those unlikely strangers who pass through our lives, and, because of serendipity or chance encounters, become integrally enmeshed in our future. One such person is Regina Sara Ryan, whom we met during the publishing of our first book; at that time we knew her only by her title, Managing Editor. Today, we think of her as a friend and literary godsend, who takes our visions and organizes them into tangible, readable thoughts. She has managed to synchronize our thinking, polish our writing, and sculpt our dreams into reality. We also applaud the staff at Hohm Press, whose dedication brought this book to fruition. We thank them dearly.

Mostly, we thank Divine Intervention, which continues to place us where we need to be, when we need to be there, and moves us forward even when we feel like standing still.

Contents

Introduction   xi

Chapter 1: Wake Up! This Is What You're Up Against   1

Chapter 2: Love Your Teenager   8

Chapter 3: The Moral Compass: All About Respect   12

Chapter 4: Their Responsibilities ... And Yours   23

Chapter 5: Teen Anxiety   33

Chapter 6: Respect, Respect, Respect   48

Chapter 7: Behavior and Consequences   51

Chapter 8: You Own Their Stuff   60

Chapter 9: Lies, Lies and Lies   67

Chapter 10: All About Manipulation   72

Chapter 11: Socialization and Safety   87

Chapter 12: Privacy ... or Not?   98

Chapter 13: Boundaries   107

Chapter 14: Your Adolescent's Health   123

Chapter 15: Academic Needs   129

Chapter 16: Serious Trouble   137

Chapter 17: A Family Epic   143

Epilogue   155

Resources for Parents and Teens   156

Bibliography   161

Index   163

About the Authors   174

Introduction

There is no deeper love than that of a parent for a child, and it is no surprise that such love is given in all its purity, and generally without bounds. What is a surprise is how quickly this small child, once your staunchest supporter, begins to pull away from you as adolescence approaches. This desperate struggle toward independence is inevitable, yet its vengeance is unexpected, leaving heartache and turmoil in its path. Welcome to the mysterious, dramatic and chaotic world of your teenager! It is during this time that parents must give their children a safe harbor, even from themselves, and wait patiently until their adolescents reestablish equilibrium and emerge as fully grown adults.

We believe that every child has the right to childhood happiness. But, they are not entitled to this right without some concessions, bound by societal rules and regulations and the structure of parental guidance. Love is simply not enough. Parenting a teenager is serious business and cannot be left to serendipity.

The advice and instruction offered in *You Don't Know Anything...!* is meant to provide you with a mooring until the seas of teenage rebelliousness and emotions quiet down. These are tumultuous times, *and* we want to reassure you that, like everything else, they will pass.

We know there are some days when you feel like you are barely holding on. As parents, you can expect to encounter trying times, some worse than others, during these next several years. Depending on the personality traits of your child, you can almost predict the degree of upheaval that may shift your life into overdrive. If your child has always been more easygoing and flexible, he or she will probably experience fewer difficulties in these teen years than a child who has always been headstrong and rebellious. Still, it is the rare child who escapes the turbulence of adolescence. Many parents agree that they feel as though they are living in a nightmare, having gone to sleep the guardian of a sweet, innocent, enthusiastic and familiar boy or girl and awakening to a barely recognizable, sullen and disrespectful, overgrown, unruly stranger.

We will be using words such as "adolescent," "teenager," "offspring" and "child" interchangeably, although by strict definition their meanings may vary, particularly with regard to age. However, it is our view that during the teen years nothing can be defined strictly; this passage is marked by blurs of time, shades of age, and brushstrokes of dreams. In *You Don't Know Anything...!: A Manual for Parenting Your Teenagers*, we will take into consideration those ages between twelve and eighteen, ending at the general time at which most teens matriculate to college or independent living, although twenty years of age is more commonly thought of as the demarcation into adulthood.

The teen years are filled with many intellectual and physiological changes involving growth spurts, developmental achievements, the appearance of secondary sex characteristics and questions of sexual identity. Equally as important, but less often mentioned, is the recognition that adolescence is also a time of "feeling" unparalleled in any other stage. Your son or daughter is feeling the possibilities that exist in a world just opening up to him or her and suffering the fears that come with breaking away from the warm dependency of the core family to venture into the unknown. Your child's adolescence will be marked by the longing to turn back to simpler times without responsibility, together with the urge to march forward, armed with little more than dreams of what might be. This book is designed to encourage in you a deeper appreciation of their challenges.

Parenting a teenager can be frustrating as well as frightening, and we will caution you throughout the chapters that follow to not lose sight of the wonderful person your child remains underneath his or her newly developed smart-aleck exterior. If you are frightened, know that he is terrified; if you are confused by some of her behavior, understand that she is totally bewildered by her words and actions. Adolescence is not representative of the person your child is destined to become; your sons and daughters are simply trying to find their way through a maze of hormones and peer pressure.

We agree that it is difficult not to feel betrayed by your teenagers when they seem indifferent to your presence, or as they shut you out of their lives altogether. At the same time, we encourage you not to react childishly, pushing your offspring away in the same manner. Your teenagers need you as much now as they ever have. If you are steadfast in your belief that your children are wonderful, despite their behaviors to the contrary; if you continue to find the good in them, even when they are behaving badly; they will have exactly what they need to make it through this challenging period. They will have *you*.

The Team Approach

As we talk about your teenagers' tumultuous behavior, the focus of this book may appear to be negatively slanted, when, in fact, it is only the behavior that is negative. The teaching tools included in these pages are intended to help you learn how to form boundaries and enforce consequences. We urge you to view these tools in a positive light, as they will pave the way for new and more constructive behaviors for both you and your teenager.

You are reading this book because of your concern for your child, *and* probably also because your parenting methods have been unsuccessful in the past. We are trained and skilled in identifying and redirecting your child's behavior, and because we are not emotionally conjoined with your child, we can offer assistance without the interference of self-doubt or guilt. You, on the other hand, have something to offer that we cannot: You have the ability to love and nurture your child. Together, we can formulate a well-constructed plan for success: *We* can provide the parenting guidelines as long as *you* provide the consistency and unconditional love. Together, this team cannot fail. However, to insure the success of our plan, you must commit to *like* your child, particularly when he or she is impossibly unlikable, and to parent consistently according to the guidelines we are about to share with you. This will take hard work, but the rewards you reap will be well worth it.

Our Work with Teens

Treating patients in a "safe" setting, in our office practice, we've been privileged to witness family dynamics from a clinical rather than an academic perspective. We have seen firsthand the ways in which couples perceive each other and react or shut down because of their perceptions. We've had a bird's-eye view of children and how they "fit" into a family, of how they perceive their position in the family, of the underpinnings of sibling rivalry, of caustic parents, and of feelings of unworthiness and betrayal. We doubt that there is any arena in which emotions are as volatile and raw, as pure yet contaminated, as truthful yet deceitful as in family therapy. In our practice, these emotions are expressed without fear of retribution, finally relieving the hidden anguish and anxieties that both parents and teens have held within.

Our clinical practice has spanned more than twenty-three years, during which we have evaluated and treated virtually hundreds of teenagers and their families. Some teens have come to us voluntarily, hoping to solve their family problems or to achieve a greater understanding of themselves; some have been dragged in by their frustrated parents, who demand to know how to fix the "problem" child. Some have been ordered to our office by the court system for treatment after committing a crime, or as a victim of their own intense anger and rage, in a proactive attempt at restructuring their behavior. Regardless of whether these teens have come in willingly, reluctantly, or with defiance, they have all come to us proficient at masking their true feelings and hiding their innermost fears, and needing acceptance and love.

We have parented four children, now adults. We understand that it is not easy to raise a teenager in today's society, with its breakdown of social norms and moral values and the ever-present loyalty to peer pressure. Each of our children has a unique personality, and therefore they could not be understood, assisted, or disciplined alike. Nonetheless, there are some behaviors which, although approached somewhat differently from one teenager to another, must be adhered to without ambiguity.

As you might expect, our views have evolved over the past two decades to become finely tuned in dealing with the needs of both parents and their teenagers. While complete agreement among all parties is rare, still we have witnessed successful outcomes, time after time, based on mutual respect and consistent boundary setting. No matter how difficult your dilemma with your teen, the problems can and will be resolved if you accept the philosophy of this book and believe that all things can be solved with knowledge and love.

No one is a perfect parent; we have made mistakes and so have you. We can only strive to be the best parents we can be, believing that there is no mistake that cannot be learned from, no behavior that cannot be reversed, and no future that is etched in stone. Every family can master the passage of the teenage years successfully, and we are here to guide you with the knowledge we have gained from our personal and professional experiences.

What You Can Expect from This Book

As the parent of a teenager, you have been issued a ticket on a roller coaster ride, and you won't be exiting this amusement park any time soon. This book will be your map, as well as a source of encouragement or consolation as you take the trip.

To use another analogy, you have entered an adolescent "spin zone," where your child's lies will easily become twisted versions of the truth; where his manipulations will provide a hot-wired shortcut to secondary gains; where her lack of integrity will be a threat to the very foundation of your trust. Their race toward independence will be brutal and genetically encoded; there is no stopping it. Your pimply-faced adolescent, who is barely able to fix his own lunch, is obsessing about the opposite sex in ways that you don't even want to know. While you scurry to catch up to your teenagers' premature thrust into autonomy, they are confidently racing ahead solo, convinced that they no longer need your supervision or advice. This book will advise you in how to slow down or speed up enough to see the big picture; how to anticipate and respond to the inevitable; and how to forestall manipulation and even avoid tragedy.

As your teens' lives hang in the balance of defiance and immaturity, you will find yourself consumed in a struggle to save them. Yet, as quickly as they reach for the safety and comfort of your hand, in the next moment they push it away. *You Don't Know Anything…!* will help you to see that successful parenting is as much about hovering closely as it is about giving space. It will arm you with the knowledge you need to understand your teens and commit to stand beside and sometimes in front of them.

As the parent, *you* are the voice of reason. Our commitment in this book is to empower you in this stand, even as your teenager tries your patience and seeks omnipotence by attempting to push you off the top step of the familial ladder. The dichotomy we observe, and hope to prepare you for, is this: As much as your child attempts to avoid disharmony, he or she invites it by creating and perpetuating chaos and confusion. It's normal. This manual will provide insight into such "normal" teenage behavior, keeping in mind that although no two children are alike, many behavior patterns are common, even universal. This book will address these commonalities.

We have agreed to help you to anticipate and redirect teen behavior which is off balance, and to redirect your own thinking and behavior. We will assist you with boundary setting and consistency – guiding you to devise reasonable consequences in a fair, patient, mature and objective manner.

As we begin this work together, let us affirm that we *know* that your patience has been tested to the limits. Your child knows it as well. Our primary thesis throughout these pages is that your teenager *expects* to be called on his or her insolent behavior. If you do not do so, you contribute to their confusion with a mixture of both relief and rage. After all, as the parent, *you* are supposed to enforce the rules. When your teenage sons and daughters misbehave, they expect to be punished, although their indignation speaks otherwise. If you do not parent them during their rebellious defiance of rules, you will cause them anxiety and insecurity with the supposition that no one is in charge.

With perseverance and tenacity, a good sense of humor, and some unexpected blessings, you and your teen will eventually reach the other side of what can only be described as "the ride of your lives." Remember, your adolescent children need you to be there for them. Without exception, they cannot successfully master this challenging ride without you.

Chapter 1

Wake Up!
This Is What You're Up Against

There is no need for us to sugarcoat what you have already discovered about your teenagers; they are nothing if not selfish, self-centered, manipulative and ruthless. If this statement seems offensive, please don't take it personally. Regardless of the amount of quality time you have spent with your children, the financial sacrifices you have made, and the hopes and dreams on which you have hung your parental heart, your offspring will ooze with ingratitude. They are the sun and moon of their own universe, sprinkling their skies with stars – their friends. Your teenagers and their friends float along their own private Milky Way with little regard for your needs. Unless you come with money or a ride, you have no importance to them, as you merely reside on planet Earth.

Depending on the day or the hour, your teens' moods will vacillate between selfishness and intentional disregard for your rules as they race toward premature independence with a sense of entitlement and with their judgment lagging behind their autonomy.

Your son or daughter at this stage is the epitome of a teenager, behaving exactly as this milestone dictates. While this may be of little consolation to your injured feelings, you can take solace that adolescents are predictably unpredictable. When they disregard the rules you set, their behavior is not to be condoned, even though it is to be expected. But recognizing this life phase helps to keep everything in proper perspective. In a perfect world, your children would be appreciative of your efforts and eternally grateful for your sacrifices, of which there have been and will continue to be many; in their world, they stand alone in their grandiosity, searching for instant gratification with an insatiable need for more.

During this stage your child is encoded by nature to march to a different drum; he or she needs your assistance to find the balance between what they need and what they want. You find yourself on high alert as their world becomes riddled with risk-taking behavior, heightened by soaring emotions on one hand and plummeting despair on the other. Your teenager's sense of reasoning is littered with skewed perceptions, where monumental decisions are made by a simple roll of the dice.

Back to the Good Ole Days?
To be sure, there are times you will wish you could turn back the clock and start over. In your daydreams you may find yourself lying by a swimming pool sipping a cool drink and reading magazines without a care in the world. In this wonderful scenario you are responsible for absolutely nothing, and in charge of absolutely no one. You drift off with only one thought: This is the life you were intended to live.

Wake up! That dream is twelve or fifteen years off; you have produced offspring, and you are stuck with them. Now, you have to figure out what to do with them. We know you're feeling overwhelmed and fed up with your children's indignation and sarcasm, their comments directed toward you muttered under their breath purposefully loud enough for you to hear. No one could have prepared you for this stage of your life, nor theirs; yet here you are, staring into the face of someone who pretends to be your child, and whom you do not like. They may call you Mom and Dad convincingly, yet they cannot possibly be yours, especially when they challenge you in the war of wills, finger-pointing at your inept parenting skills, unearthing your secret insecurities.

You on Trial

When you have teenagers residing under your roof, expect long and sleepless nights, kept awake with nagging doubts of your parenting abilities – doubts planted by your offspring.

It is astonishing how quickly a teenager is able to convince you that you have no idea what you are doing, until you retaliate by losing control. Then, he or she has succeeded in gaining control. Later, in the quiet of night, as your overgrown child lies sleeping, you tearfully question how you have come to this point, pitted against your teenager in a battle in which you did not enlist. Words spoken in anger illuminate the darkness, robbing you of much-needed sleep.

You don't want it to be this way: all the negative energy that has filled your once-harmonious home; this festering of negative emotions demonstrating the enormous power of your teenage son or daughter, with exhausting escapades and screaming matches their only method of communication, or, what's even worse, their unbearable silence. You have a sense of longing for your once-loving child in all his or her innocence, relying on you for the answers to their questions, finding comfort when you soothed their fears. Now you find yourself plotting to decode their secrets, hypervigilant as you gather clues to stall their emotional destruction.

When you weren't looking, your teenagers have become undercover sleuths, amassing evidence to prove their accusations against you, adept at turning the tables as they smokescreen their own deficiencies by pointing out yours. You will find yourself in the witness chair as they become the self-appointed judge and jury of your infractions, supporting their allegations with erroneous evidence, cleverly taking your words out of context for the purpose of turning them against you. You foolishly plead for mercy when your son callously has none to give; your words are manipulated with innuendos of nothing resembling the truth. Or your daughter's closing argument proves brilliant as she gains her own sympathy at having had the misfortune of being born to a family such as yours. This is what you're up against, without much hope for logic to speak in your defense.

While you attempt to rise above your teenagers' faulty rhetoric and skewed perceptions to a place where truth and reason prevail, it is senseless to remind them of your monetary sacrifices or emotional endeavors. They can't hear you right now. Any proof you enter as evidence will be rejected as irrelevant. There is only one issue at hand, and that issue is the constraints that you have placed upon them with the sole purpose of ruining their life. The gavel resounds with their ruling: You have been found guilty.

You plead, to no avail. You request an appeal; denied. Your teenagers have encased themselves behind a soundproof, invisible

About Sheila

Sheila came to the office with her fourteen-year-old daughter, Ashley. From Ashley's authoritative tone as she spoke to her mother in the waiting room, it was immediately clear to us who was "in charge" of whom. In fact, once inside the therapy room, daughter Ashley held nothing back when it came to listing her mother's foibles, while Mother sank into her chair, embarrassed by Ashley's accusations of her inability to make a "decent family meal." When Sheila finally tried to speak in her own defense, Ashley quickly cited example after example of what she considered to be her mother's inadequate parenting skills. The room soon grew quiet due to Mother's surrender. It was torturous to witness such a browbeating.

shield and entered the ethers of adolescence, where adults are prohibited. This is the stance from which you will parent from now until they reach adulthood.

You are on the outside, looking in.

Step One: The Business of Parenting

Separating your feelings from entanglement with those of your teenagers and separating your feelings from your convictions and decisions is the most difficult part of any ordeal with them. Try to think of parenting as a notebook page divided into two separate columns, one labeled "The Emotional Aspect" and the other "The Business Aspect." The Emotional Aspect consists of love, hope, laughter, sadness, trepidation and tears. The Business Aspect must be devoid of these emotions in order to function objectively, and includes a blueprint, a job description, goals, incentives, bonuses, rewards and consequences. It is this *business* of parenting that is so difficult, yet so essential to the overall emotional well-being of your children. If only love were enough.

The original complaint that brought Ashley and her mother to therapy was Ashley's angry assaults on her family. It was no wonder to us that Ashley was allowed to manipulate the family with her demands, as there was no parent who could rein in her smokescreening behavior.

When we confronted Ashley about her disrespect, reminding her that her misbehavior in school was the reason for the scheduled visit, she became sullen and quiet. It took almost six months for Ashley to respect the new boundaries that Sheila learned to make, but once Ashley realized that she could not walk all over her mother, she began to display more respectful behavior, not only at home but also at school.

Robert's Dreams

Robert had dreams of being rich. He didn't care how it happened, just *that* it happened. Although he was a senior in high school, he hadn't learned much about buckling down to get his assignments completed, nor did he apply good study habits with homework. The results were barely average grades at school and complaints that he was being singled out by his teachers and unjustly accused of having a poor academic attitude.

Robert's parents had spent most of their son's junior high and high school years championing his complaints, often coming to parent/teacher conferences to express their disappointment that the teacher had not given Robert better grades on essay tests and reports. Over the years, Robert had done a masterful job persuading his parents of his teachers' injustices. Now Mom and Dad were concerned that because of the teachers' inability to see Robert's potential, he would not be accepted to an Ivy League College.

It was difficult to break up the collusion that had blinded Robert's parents from the truth: Their son had not applied himself during his academic years, and was now looking for his parents to bail him out, as they always had. In this case, we felt it was more important for Robert to understand the valuable lesson of hard work, which is the straight line to making dreams a reality. In order to do that, we had to convince the parents to see exactly what was going on: that they had become enablers to Robert's dream of the "easy life." After some work with Robert, and a lot less enabling from his parents, the young man began to reflect back on his academic years with a healthy remorse.

All was not lost. Robert was accepted into a local community college, where hard work earned him good grades. The outcome was acceptance to the college of his choice at the end of his sophomore year.

In the business of parenting there is much to do. Behaviors have to be divided into those that are acceptable and those that are unacceptable. There are goals to set, parameters to outline, boundaries to form, lessons to teach and consequences to enforce. You must act under this business plan, setting aside your feelings, while your children learn to move forward within those boundaries in a healthy and safe manner.

We are great supporters of dreams and crusaders of the human spirit. But neither dreams nor spirit will come to fruition for your children without you identifying their manipulations and deterring their poor decisions.

In doing this "business," you are embarking upon uncharted territory, an obstacle course which keeps your footing unsure. Your path is muddy and does not allow retreat, so you must trudge forward through the muck until you reach the other side. There is simply no other way.

Chapter 2

Love Your Teenager

We do not know you, nor do we know anything about the stages of your own life, the hardships you may be enduring, the isolation you may feel. We are not insensitive to your needs, but right now the needs of your teenagers are paramount; their needs must come first.

During this very narrow window of time, your son or daughter will speed through the maturation process, growing from a dependent young child into an adult in little more than a decade. Then, even if they negotiate this passage unsuccessfully, they will be thrust into the world without the parental cushion to fall back on, expected by society to behave like an adult with full-fledged responsibilities.

We are all the sum total of our experiences, and your teenagers are no exception. What they pack into their emotional suitcase today will accompany them for the rest of their lives; it is your responsibility to ensure that this baggage is not laden down with insults and criticisms, unhappiness and defeat. Your teenagers deserve your support as you envision their potential, even when it has been obliterated by their poor choices and bad behavior. If their suitcases are full, help empty them.

The Idea of Love, and the Reality
We have encountered parents in our practice who love their children very much, yet possess very little ability to demonstrate that love in a manner their sons or daughters understand; in the end, their teens may well go into the world carrying suitcases empty of all but self-loathing.

Sweet Janice

Janice came into the office with a sugary sweet disposition, which, upon closer scrutiny, we recognized as a cover for her repressed anger. For the first three months of therapy, she was unable to get in touch with any real feelings, other than to say she just felt unhappy but she didn't know why. As time passed, she began looking forward to her therapy appointments, always bringing in test results or report cards, pages from her diary, or "love " notes from her boyfriend. Her mother seemed jealous and threatened. She would make comments to us like, "I don't know why she can't share these things with me. After all, I'm her parent, not you."

In family therapy, Janice was brave enough to answer her mother's question by exposing her sadness about her mother's "practical and mechanical" behavior. Janice admitted feeling disappointed in herself whenever she confided in her mother because she felt that her mother inferred that nothing Janice did was good enough. Through her tears, Janice addressed her mother, telling her, "You just never really listened. When I was sad, you never hugged me; you just told me that if that was the only problem I had I should consider myself lucky."

Janice's mother also had tears as she confessed her awkwardness in giving kisses and hugs, especially as her children got older. "My parents weren't much for hugging and kissing, so I guess I learned to parent the same way," she told us.

It took some time for Janice and her mother to begin to bond on a more emotional level, but a year later Janice's demeanor was no longer superficially sweet. She appeared genuinely happier, especially since everyone in the family seemed to have benefited from therapy and was beginning to realize the necessity of emotional bonding between parents and children.

You must be able to give your teenager what he or she needs using words and actions that clearly depict love. He needs hugs and kisses, support and kindness. She needs you to cry with her, laugh with her, encourage her to lean on you, praise her successes, and allow her to fail. Even if you have not been that parent in the past, it is not too late to begin. Erase all of your preconceived notions about parenting, the manner in which you were supported or disapproved of by your own parents, and think for yourself. You know what your child needs, and you know you must be the parent he or she needs you to be. Those of you who have entered adulthood with your own suitcases filled with unresolved childhood issues should seek professional help to empty them lest they spill onto your teenager, contaminating their childhood with sins they did not commit.

Your adolescents need to know you love them not only when they are good, but especially when they are not. Your own flexibility or rigidity, as well as your childhood experiences, will ultimately determine how you will parent your child and the manner in which you will react when things go wrong.

Our Parents, Ourselves

No matter how much you wish it were not so, you may recognize more similarities between yourself and your parents than you care to admit. Don't be surprised when your child tests you to the limit and your parents' words fall from your mouth. When you least expect it, you will hear yourself saying, "Because I said so, that's why," and you will have come full circle. As much as this phrase drove you crazy when your parents said it, as much as you vowed you would never torment your children with this statement, when you are pushed beyond your own patience, these seem the only appropriate words to say. In fleeting glimpses, we see that we have become our parents.

Rather than rebelling against your own childhood issues, embrace those parental teachings that you can now appreciate as an adult, and toss aside those that were hurtful or unfair. Open your mind to the fact that your offspring are finding their way along a rocky path, much the same as you did in your adolescence, making similar mistakes, the result of similar poor choices. Although you are going to have to be firm in your directives, you are also going to have to cut them some slack and pick and choose your battles. It won't be long before they will leave the nest, and you will give anything for one more day of their presence.

Chapter 3

The Moral Compass: All About Respect

The teenage passage is not without scars. Often parents have a desire to "rescue" their children, hoping to insulate them from painful experiences. This is not only unrealistic, but it interferes with your teenager's ability to learn how to make better decisions, develop coping skills, and prioritize those things most important in life. Allowing your son or daughter to make their own mistakes is part of separating, and this, of course, is the most difficult part of parenting a teenager.

It is difficult to discard the early years of bedtime stories and goodnight kisses; those times were as important to your children then as giving them space and responsibility is now. Before you allow them to wander too far away from the proverbial apron strings, they must be in possession of a blueprint of life, created by both of you. That blueprint must include the basic principles of manners, decision making, ethics and conduct based upon the value system and moral philosophy that is fundamental in your family. Though these values are individualized and unique to your family, they also serve as a moral compass to most families. For example, the right to be safe from physical or emotional pain is a universal standard, as are integrity, trust, forthrightness, and compassion for the human condition. Many of these standards cannot simply be taught by verbal instruction, but rather must be transmitted through modeling and imprinting. If your behavior is one of respect for others, it is likely your teenager will adopt that philosophy as well.

Drawing the Line, with Respect

When your children were much younger, you taught them not to say anything hurtful to others, even though such comments were spoken in innocence. Similarly, your teenager does not have the right to blurt out hurtful comments but should be expected to use common sense and courtesy as a guide.

Some teens will go out of their way to make especially hurtful and derogatory comments to their parents. Yet these same parents, who so carefully taught earlier lessons to their young children, seem inept at teaching them to their teenagers. Instead, they shoulder the brunt of their teens' hurtful remarks under the auspices that an adolescent needs to vent angry emotions.

This faulty thinking does a disservice to both of you. If your child has that much pent up anger and aggression, perhaps he or she is in need of counseling to unravel the underpinnings of their rage. Let us all agree that your children, regardless of age, should not be encouraged to utter every thought that comes into their heads without some type of censoring ability and impulse control.

For example, it is not within the standard of acceptable verbiage to announce to one's parents that they are hated, or stupid, or that they are wished dead. If your adolescent is angry at a punishment you have issued, he or she may vent their feelings and displeasure in the privacy of their room, or to their friends out of earshot and without your knowledge. But to announce such feelings to you directly, or simply in your presence, is disrespectful and should not be tolerated. Name-calling is a sign of immaturity (which is to be expected) and disrespect (which is not). If you do not execute a consequence, you are doing your teenager a disservice by being a lazy parent. Disrespect is a form of misbehavior that should be identified and dealt with rapidly and without negotiation.

Adam and Cheryl

As soon as the Schneider family entered therapy we knew it was going to take some major restructuring to define each parent's role with relation to their two children, Adam and Cheryl, ages fourteen and fifteen respectively. From the moment the parents began an attempt to relay to us what they believed the problems were in the household, Adam began talking over his father, accusing him of "not having a clue" what he was talking about. Cheryl chimed in, saying, "Both our parents are so lame, it's ridiculous that we even have to be here." Then both teens agreed they had better things to do with their time than to spend it in a therapy session.

Mr. and Mrs. Schneider shrugged their shoulders helplessly and said, "You see, this is what we have to put up with."

We told the teens that we were here to assist the family to learn better methods of communicating with each other, methods that were based on respect and common courtesy. They looked blank, and bored, until we got their attention by saying, "If your parents agree, all of you will be spending one hour each week with us, working on your ability to be more pleasant and courteous."

The teens were shocked that someone had dared to challenge their authority; certainly their parents had little

In our opinion, respect is one of the four cornerstones of behavior, along with trust, kindness and integrity. Without these cornerstones, there is nothing solid upon which a strong foundation can be built, and without a foundation, your child's behavior will have no base for positive growth and development.

The rules of conduct are made not by us but by society, and observing them – or failing to observe them – will determine your child's future. Disrespect in school today may only get capability of setting boundaries with regard to the manner in which they were spoken to. We identified those areas that we believed constituted respectful conversation and those that did not. The siblings were quick to accuse us of forcing them to "act fake" and of not allowing them to say what was on their minds.

The Schneiders looked to us for guidance, as they were about to be manipulated by the very idea that their children should be able to speak aloud anything that was on their minds, to the detriment of others. We explained to the teenagers that their ideas and concerns were not being "shut down," but that the way in which they approached their conversation was to be reworked. For the next three weeks Adam and Cheryl rebelled at this new style of respectful conversation, until we announced the creation of a behavior chart that would assist them in "remembering" how to speak with their parents. Within one week of upholding consequences that were the direct result of disrespect, both Schneider teens quickly changed their tunes; although they did not like having to modify what had become a game of putting their parents on the defensive, they disliked being without their privileges more. The Schneider adults continued in therapy for several more months while they gained some much-needed parenting skills.

your teenager one hour in study hall, but in the vast arena of life, their disrespect may one day cost them their employment or their marriage.

We have all stood in the presence of someone who has spoken their mind to the detriment of others, ignorantly displaying bias or gender harassment, and we have all pondered their upbringing. That adult is *your child* if you do not curtail their insistence on saying every hurtful comment that pops into their head.

No Debates, Please

Of course, children do not appreciate being corrected on their behavior; they take deep offense when they are not entitled to say and do whatever they please. *That is too bad.* If you, or a teacher or police officer, or any other person in authority issues a directive, it is to be followed; end of story!

Teenagers love a good debate, and will take the opportunity whenever it avails itself. If you allow your child to debate your decisions, you are sending the incorrect message that you and they are equal on a level playing field. You are not. This is not a competition; therefore, when you declare a conversation is finished, the subject is over.

Teenagers should not be invited to enter into any type of

Mary's Story

From an early age Mary had an uncanny ability to "see through" explanations she was given by her parents. By the time she had matriculated to junior high school her debating expertise was known throughout her family and among friends and teachers. In fact, Mary was so bright that she argued just to argue, finding fun in winning, often at the expense of humiliating those around her. When the school suggested she come into therapy, Mary was thrilled at the prospect of a new arena in which to flaunt her skills. If we suggested she come to therapy once weekly, she cited examples of therapy working more efficiently on a twice-weekly basis; if she was asked to express her thoughts and feelings, she gave chapter and verse on her "trust issues," accusing us of trying to take advantage of her vulnerabilities. She had managed to bamboozle herself by intellectualizing every thought, question, sentence or request made by anyone, until she isolated herself into an audience of one.

debate with you, nor should lengthy defensive explanations be given when the outcome of a decision is not favorable to your child. The oldest trick in the book is to force a change of mind with manipulation – wearing you down and confusing you until you can no longer remember the premise of your ideas or the manner in which you reached your conclusion. This trickery is aimed at undermining your parental role. The opinions of your teenagers are often invaluable when asked for, but your adolescent son or daughter has no business butting into any adult conversation uninvited and uninformed.

Further, if your teen demands to know how you came to your conclusion about an issue, you should not make them privy to the details surrounding your decision. Unless their safety is at

The fact was that Mary felt inadequate in comparison to her older sibling, who had always been the apple of their parents' eye. Mary quickly recognized that although she did not have the talents her brother had, she could capitalize on the one talent she did have. If attention was what Mary was seeking, she found it by aggravating and humiliating others, once again confirming that negative attention is better than no attention at all.

Although Mary's parents did not mean to favor their son, and, in fact did not admit to it, Mary's perceptions, right or wrong, led to her developing a way to gain her parents' attention. Through therapy, the parents began rewarding Mary for good behavior and disciplining her for any type of conversational behavior that was argumentative and demeaning. Her teachers were made aware of the plan and cooperated in the classroom setting.

The outcome was successful once Mary's parents realized that every thought a teenager has does not have to be spoken if that thought is detrimental to the health or happiness of others.

stake, to include them in lengthy conversations is to cast them into the role of co-adult.

Parents of young children are capable of issuing directives such as "Never run into the street" without question and following up with a severe consequence if that directive isn't followed. Yet, those same parents cannot enforce a directive to their teenager, allowing it to be debated or ignored.

We want to yell out, "What is wrong with you? Why can't you be as certain, now that your child is older, about the dangers that lurk about? Why don't you demand the respect you deserve? Where have you gone wrong and what are you going to do about it?"

No Democracy

The questions posed above are all good ones, and the answers may be more apparent once we clear up one of our favorite issues. Without clarity about this topic we might just as well throw up our hands in despair and turn our teenagers loose into society unplugged. The important distinction to be etched indelibly in your brain is this: Your family is not a democracy. That's right, we said it! Further, your family should not be run by the impulsive, outrageous opinions of people less informed and less experienced than you. You have earned your right to be the adult through your own maturation process, and your children do not rank on a par with you. They never will.

Regardless of your children's ages or education, you are the parent and the adult; that makes you the head of the hierarchy in your family for all time. Try as they might, your children cannot hope to obtain that status until the day you take your final breath. Even senility outranks coming-of-age children, since pearls of wisdom can still be harvested through the fog of dementia.

If you question the importance of the hierarchy platform, think of any functioning group and examine its underpinnings. Whether it is a religion, a political movement, or a neighborhood town meeting, every organized group has a leader, elected or appointed, and basic rules to be followed. Your family is no different. No one expects your children to live under a dictatorship, but neither should you live under the threat of tyranny, mutiny or treason.

To be a teenager is to be engaged in a power struggle involving a winner and a loser; if you are not certain of your position as head of your household, you will be easily upended by your power-hungry teen. Make your directives fair and decisive and you will have nothing to explain to your offspring.

Admit Mistakes and Guard Your Tongue

There may be times when you have not been fair – times when you made your decisions based upon anger and emotional volatility. If this is the case, you need to rectify the situation immediately. It is one thing to issue a fair decision and quite another to project your hostilities onto your child. Children will have great respect for a parent who admits he or she was wrong. They will see it as an act of bravery and take a lesson from an excellent role model. To see a parent as imperfect is to see a parent who is human. Apologizing for an oversight or an angry outburst and reassessing your teen's request in their favor will be appreciated and remembered.

There are some parents who are afraid to admit failure, who see failing as a weakness, and believe that making a mistake means being vulnerable. There is no shame in making a mistake; the shame lies only in the pretense of perfection. Children who believe their parent is perfect are doomed to failure. Instinctively knowing they will never be able to attain perfection, they will embrace defeat. Perfection or the pretense of perfection causes anxiety and unhappiness for everyone, to no good end. Let your imperfection be seen and use it to your advantage; an apology from a parent is its own lesson in humility.

19

Stanley's Opinions

Stanley was offended at being brought into therapy by his parents. "I don't see what the problem is. *I decide* when my curfew is, and *I decide* what my bedtime is. Nobody tells them [pointing to his parents] when to go to bed," he said. "How would they like it if I decided *their* bedtime?"

Stanley was unable to grasp the fact that since he did not make rules for his parents, he was expected to abide by the rules that they made for him. Yet, he did not have trouble adhering to the rules of therapy. If he was told to come to a scheduled appointment, he drove himself to the appointment on time. If he was asked to write a letter to his friend who had betrayed him, he did it without the least objection. He did not feel comfortable trying to upend the therapy agenda because he was unfamiliar with the arena; he recognized his place as the "patient" and not the doctor.

In his household, Stanley had been given "equal rights" with

It goes without saying that your teenagers should never be compared to their friends or siblings; they are individuals who have been born with gifts and talents that are uniquely theirs. While disrespectful conduct may tempt you to make a comparison out of frustration, or during an angry outburst, check yourself and make sure that no matter how hard you have to bite your tongue, not a word spills out that sounds like you wish your child was more like someone else.

There will be plenty of trying times, and innumerable tests of your endurance, but words spoken can never be taken back, and they hurt. If you have made this mistake in the past, it is not too late to rectify the situation. Go back and apologize, not only to the child who feels "inferior" but to the one against whom you have measured your unmanageable teen. Both have regard to his place in the family. He had been asked what he wanted to wear, what he wanted to eat, and where he wanted to go from the age when he first began to understand human speech. It was little wonder, then, that he could not discern the difference between being the parent and the child once he became a teenager, where his decisions could not be left to his own desires.

There were many setbacks in therapy, as Stanley's parents were continually willing to negotiate with their son rather than sticking to their parental plan. With each inconsistency Stanley became empowered and therapy had to begin again, with several steps backward. But because of their frustration, Stanley's parents eventually made enough of a commitment to therapy that they were able to stand their ground and begin to regain their position as head of the household.

Now, two years later, although things have much improved, Stanley still missteps every so often, almost as if to test his parents' ability to follow through.

suffered or feel guilty because of your comments, and both will resent the other in years to come if this situation isn't remedied.

But how about when the shoe is on the other foot? What about the way you feel when your son or daughter does not want to speak with you, or avoids being with you, muttering derogatory comments about your character? Aside from the fact that this behavior is disrespectful, it is also hurtful. We call this behavior "parental rejection." During normal teenage phases, your children will displace their anger and frustrations on the safest person, and often the target of their agitation is a parent. It doesn't feel good to you, and, truthfully, it doesn't feel good to them, but because of their immaturity they often cannot control the impulse to lash out and hurt someone.

One reason your teens choose to lash out at home is because you have given them your unconditional love, and as much as they are disappointed by their own behavior, they are also pretty sure you are never going to turn your back on them, or stop loving them. That is what parents are called to do – love their children when they are most unlovable.

When you have been hurt by your son or daughter, you must resist the urge to retaliate. If you hurl insults back, they will be forever scarred by your words, even if they were only said in anger. As the adult in this situation, it is up to you to control your temper. Know that your teenager loves you, and forgive their immaturity. That does not mean overlook the immaturity; this behavior still warrants a consequence. But let your adolescent know that you do not hold against them what they have said to you. They will look back on these days with astonishment, wondering how you could have loved them when it seemed no one else could.

Chapter 4

Their Responsibilities ...
and Yours

A s an adult, you often find yourself overwhelmed with life tasks, not the least of which is raising children, plus managing a career, doing housework, scheduling carpooling, and taking care of financial responsibilities. It isn't news to you that you're in need of help, but you are looking in the wrong place if you think your teenager will step forward. Nonetheless, when something's got to give, many parents enlist their children to assist in household duties, including the rearing of their younger siblings. If you are looking for conflict, you can find it right here.

No Exploitation
Your teenagers want nothing to do with *your* responsibilities, nor should they. Their job is to attend school, get good grades, socialize, and eventually learn enough to matriculate into society. This is not to say they shouldn't have chores, but by "chores" we mean light housework, such as cleaning their bedrooms, and responsibilities which may include mowing the lawn or taking out the garbage. A chore is of the nature of lending a hand, with some degree of accountability, some degree of prioritizing, and some degree of accomplishment upon completion. In our opinion, unless you and your teens have worked out some type of work arrangement where you are paying them a salary to do a job for which they have interviewed, you are exploiting them.

We are adamant about our position on exploitation. Your son or daughter needs to have time for those things that are important in defining their adolescence; housework is not one of those things. If you need a little help with sweeping the floor, they should be asked to pitch in, but to assign them *your* jobs, just because you can, is both unfair and an abuse of power.

Your teenagers have their own set of responsibilities. They must attend school, study for exams, write research papers, be

Angry John

John was one of the more angry teenagers we have seen in our practice, and for good reason. His father, a single parent raising his son, didn't believe he should have to go to work and then come home to keep the house. He put responsibility for most of the housework and almost all of the cooking on John's shoulders. Admittedly, Mr. R. wasn't the neatest man in the world, so even if the housework was done in a slipshod manner it didn't come under white-glove scrutiny. Nonetheless, it was up to John to make sure the garbage went to the street on pickup days, the grocery shopping was done, something was made for dinner, and there was enough soda and beer in the refrigerator.

John's mother died when he was still in grade school, and he tried to help his father out as best he could because he didn't want his father to be sad. John felt extremely sad at the loss of his mother, but he could tell that the overall atmosphere of the house was "nicer" when he did his part to pick up his clothing or walk the dog.

Over the years, as John got bigger so did the list of chores; in fact, little by little, his father gave him more and more responsibility for home maintenance, both inside and outside, until John was handling the majority of the tasks. That left little time for studies, and almost no time for socialization. John prepared for pop quizzes, make friends, find a date, socialize, join organizations, excel in sports, have a talent, play the piano or the tuba, come home, do homework, make a snack and sometimes dinner, organize their clothing, worry about being included in parties, outings, movies, and overnights, make money, lose privileges, gain them back . . . and see to a multitude of other developmental "tasks."

was isolated from his peers because of his "job" and felt like an outsider in his classes. By the time he was a junior in high school, he had had enough, and he snapped. He began lashing out, starting fights among his classmates, and ending up in the principal's office at least once a week. Then John beat up a boy one year his junior and put him in the hospital. The boy's parents pressed assault charges, and John was ordered by the court to therapy for anger management.

After several sessions, it became clear that John's anger was displaced from his father onto his peers. It also became clear that John had become a "parentified" child after his mother died, meaning that he took it upon himself to parent his remaining parent, rather than his remaining parent parenting him. Because he was not given grief counseling, nor any opportunity to talk about his mother and resolve his feelings about her death, John's feelings of loss, coupled with his anger toward his father for his father's lack of understanding and exploitation, brought the situation to a very serious head.

John's father agreed to hear what we had to say but defended his right to "make" his teenager "help out" around the house. To date, John continues to express his sadness and his anger in a more constructive manner by verbalizing it, but, unfortunately, his father has not given John the emotional support he craves.

Socialization – Their Vital Work

If you were going to measure the worth of your offspring by how little they did around the house, you would be sadly disappointed. Teenagers are busy with their own lives, and although superficially that life may seem nothing more than hanging out with friends, every social interaction is a building block toward the understanding of human relationships. Socialization is as vital to relationships as academics is to learning, because one without the other makes a very one-dimensional young adult. Through interaction with peers, teenagers sharpen their powers of observation, test the limits of their grandiose behavior, find the courage to speak in a group, look for someone with whom to share confidences and trust, and, eventually, seek a partner with whom they can share the rest of their life.

While socialization comes easily for some young people, it is difficult and emotionally painful for others. If your child is shy or introverted, if their self-esteem and self-confidence is less than adequate, you may observe them watching from the sidelines, as if they are disinterested in making friends or participating in school functions. Trust us; they are interested. They just don't have the necessary coping skills to take risks, or the emotional confidence to bounce back if they are rejected. Your son or daughter very much wants to be sought out by their peers, picked to be on the team, romantically involved with someone who bolsters their confidence level. They just don't always know how to get there.

Times Have Changed

Life is so much more complicated than it was at an earlier time when there were few expectations beyond helping with the family chores and contributing to the family workload. In years gone by, the primary emphasis was not on socializing or dating, schoolwork or recreation, but on survival: bringing in the crops before the first winter freeze, tending the cattle, milking the cows, hoping the chickens would lay eggs. If these tasks were not handled, there would be no food, and families would starve. Success was measured not in material possessions, of which there were very few, but in the unity of family: sharing experiences of birth and death, working side by side with a sense of pride and loyalty as an integral member of a tight-knit unit.

In this twenty-first century, materialism has all but snuffed out intangible successes, which have been overshadowed by the "me" society of insatiable appetites fueled by greed and jealousy. Rather than working side by side, people are pitted against each other in fierce competition, vying for jobs and lying for money, which has become the barometer by which our young people have learned to measure success and is the underpinning of anger and depression.

The love of money has become the driving force behind the seventy-hour work week, robbing our children of precious time. Employers foster the notion that everyone is expendable, and in such a competitive world anyone who is unwilling to play by the company rules is simply replaced by someone who will.

For all of our cumulative intelligence and technological progress, we have surged forward but left our children behind. They are being babysat by television sets, their minds captured by violence and sexually inappropriate material. They interact silently with television actors whose sarcasm or racial biases cross the airwaves, invading our children's psyches. They are being fed junk for their brains and junk for their stomachs. The dinner table is littered with crumpled bags of fast food – wads of salt and grease wrapped in pretty packaging, cooked by someone else's mother, packaged by someone else's siblings, and advertised by someone else's father.

If you take an objective look at just how much quality time you spend with your teens – getting to know who they are actually becoming rather than projecting who you believe they are – you will be pleasantly surprised at their appreciation of your interest in their hopes, dreams, ambitions and disappointments. Instead, some of you think that because you have spent exorbitant amounts of money on your kids' clothes and activities, or because their social calendar is penciled in for the rest of the year, you have fulfilled your parental duties. You have not. Because your children attend an activity after school every day does not mean they are not being neglected. There must be a balance between activities and home life, between signing up for activities and interacting with family members, between being an integral part of a club and being an integral part of a family. The rules which must be obeyed in school or sports are meant to avoid chaos and keep the activity organized and running smoothly; the rules that children learn at home are valuable lessons in life skills and understanding the human condition. The former cannot be substituted for the latter. Exposure to your heritage and culture, making memories, and bonding are the life lessons your teenagers will take with them and pass on to their children someday.

Responsibilities and the Teenage Brain

Some of you have unreasonable expectations regarding your children, acting as if they have disappointed you and squashed your dreams. You feel they have embarrassed you by problems they cannot seem to solve or poor choices they have made. Statistics now prove what we have all assumed for quite some time: Our teenagers are unable to consistently use good judgment in making decisions. There is actually a segment of brain matter which remains immature and underdeveloped until at least the age of twenty-three, meaning that even the most responsible of your offspring will make a really bad decision some of the time, and some of them may make consistently poor decisions almost all of the time.

Your children should not be given responsibilities in areas where poor choices may impact the rest of their lives. They should not, for example, be left to watch younger siblings if those children need supervision; this includes babysitting other people's children, where the teenager certainly must exercise good judgment and attentiveness at all times.

Many parents believe that the task of babysitting will teach their teenager the fundamentals of childcare as well as responsibility. This is not only dangerously faulty thinking on the part of the adult, but a careless disregard for human life. Ask any teenage babysitter and they will tell you that most of their time is spent raiding the refrigerator, rifling through drawers and cabinets, watching television, and talking on the telephone. Should an avoidable accident occur under the watch of your child, not only they, but you, will have to carry the legal and emotional burden for quite a long time, if not forever.

Every parent wants to get to the bottom of a problem, and when your child messes up, one of the first things you are likely to ask is, "What were you thinking?" The most frequent response to that question is, "I don't know." This infuriates parents, who expect their child to come up with a better explanation than that. This is generally when the parent banishes the teen to his or her bedroom to think up a better answer, promising they will not gain freedom from solitary confinement without one. The truth is, your child really *doesn't* know what they were thinking, anymore than they weighed the possibilities of disaster, or anticipated the outcome.

However, if you insist on an answer to "What were you thinking?" your teenager will come up with one that may satisfy you, not because they have been evasive all along but because they have the power of imagination and creativity and know this is the only way they will ever be let out of their room.

In fact, the realistic bottom line in their messing up is simply this: Your teenager cannot consistently make good decisions and,

Responsible Rose

Rose had always been a responsible young lady. She was community-minded, helping to build houses with Habitat for Humanity, and did her part to recycle paper and plastic to preserve the environment. She was exceptionally compassionate to the elderly, spending half the day on Saturdays delivering "meals on wheels" to homebound senior citizens. She had always been an exceptional student and had recently been chosen to tutor others who were having difficulty grasping algebra and geometry. Rose was selected to be a foreign exchange student and represent her school and community. She planned to go to college, and gathered community service points whenever she could. She had had one steady boyfriend, who excelled in both academics and sports. For Christmas the previous year she had sold crafts at a local craft fair in order to purchase a much-needed clothes dryer for her parents.

Rose had always made good decisions with forethought and planning, which is why it was such a shock when she told her parents she was five months pregnant. Rose planned on having the baby and did not want anyone to attempt to persuade her to end the pregnancy, which is why she waited so long before confiding her news. Her steady boyfriend was not ready for the constraints of marriage, and certainly not for fatherhood, so Rose came into therapy for guidance and support. Her parents accompanied her, wanting to know how this could have happened to such a responsible girl, who knew everything about abstinence, birth control and safe sex. The answer did little to lighten their burden, but it was the only answer there was: "Your daughter is only seventeen, and seventeen-year-olds do not make consistently good decisions."

moreover, rarely thinks about the consequences of any decision they have made.

Friend or Parent? Don't Confuse Your Role

Some of you might exercise your parental right to teach a lesson by withholding privileges; others might try to "buddy up" to your child, to be his or her friend, sharing stories of your own drug problems or sexual activities. *Please don't do that!* Befriending your teenage children is not going to correct their difficulties but rather will add to them. Your teens do not need you to be their friend; they need you to be their parent. The two are not interchangeable.

A friend is someone who shares intimate confidences, who expects to be treated fairly without judgment or disloyalty, who

In a newspaper article run by the Associated Press (01/08), Laurence Steinberg, a psychology professor from Temple University, said, "The teenage brain is like a car with a good accelerator but a weak brake. With powerful impulses under poor control, the likely result is a crash."

The article described Steinberg's history, noting that "He helped draft an American Psychological Association brief for a 2005 case in which the U.S. Supreme Court outlawed the death penalty for crimes committed before the age of 18. That ruling relies on the most recent research on the adolescent brain, which indicates the juvenile brain is still maturing in the teen years and reasoning and judgment are developing well into the early to mid 20's."

Justice Anthony Kennedy, writing for the 5-4 majority in the case, wrote that "juveniles are more vulnerable or susceptible to negative influences and outside pressures, including peer pressure," which determines their decision making and impulsivity in their out of control environment.

will offer objective advice and be a shoulder to cry on. A friend is someone who supports ideas with enthusiasm and is not afraid to come forward with admonishments when your thinking is off base. Your child is neither emotionally equipped, nor mature enough, to be any of these things to you, nor should they be. We're sorry to tell you this, but during their adolescent self-serving years, the only way your child wants to include you in his or her circle of friends is if you're supplying the party house and the beer.

Your teens have their own friends, people their age whom they can "hang" with, cut up with, do stupid things with, and fight with. They cannot grow up any faster than they are programmed to, and you do them an injustice by attempting to trade the role of parent for friend so they will think you're "cool."

It is our opinion that this "not friends" rule holds true throughout life. Even as the generation gap narrows, your son or daughter will *not* have experienced your life lessons, nor developed the wisdom that comes from illness, death, betrayal, and other losses that are inevitable as we age. Sitting in the bleachers is not the same as being beaten up on the field. The stadium is filled with well-wishers, but they can never achieve the same satisfaction or the same despair as the athlete in the game. In *your* life, your children are permanently seated in the bleachers; do your best for them.

Chapter 5

Teen Anxiety

Teenagers are filled with anxiety, trepidation, and downright fear, and for good reason. Your adolescent children have little control over most of their lives. They cannot schedule their own agendas, decide whether they would like to attend school on any particular day, force their peers to like them, or magically be chosen for the team. Your daughter doesn't know if she will pass her school courses, move on to the next grade, or graduate some day. Your son doesn't know if he will get a car, get a job, or get a girlfriend. He doesn't even know if he will ever have a date. Your daughter doesn't know if she will be asked to the junior prom, if she will feel embarrassed by having her menstrual period at her best friend's swim party, or if she will be the brunt of "flat chest" jokes for the remainder of her school years. Teens are anxious about whether they are destined to be short or too tall; they worry about reaching puberty and all that involves; they obsess over when they will develop secondary sex characteristics. He worries about whether his penis is too small; she frets because her breasts are too large. There is so much to worry about every single day that it is almost impossible to stuff in any more worry. Teenagers consider themselves fortunate to get through any single day unscathed; they cannot think past tomorrow.

You may believe your children don't suffer from the worries we just listed because you see them doing nothing that, in your mind, should produces stress. Their day may appear to be predicated on hanging around with seemingly little purpose and little ambition, but don't let that fool you. Teenagers are Academy Award-winning drama queens and tough guys with devil-may-care facades, skilled at masking their true feelings. To look at them is to invite envy; from your perspective they have the whole world before them, to explore and conquer. You see them as raw clay, waiting to be molded by their own hands, with the sky their only limit. Yet, they seem unaware of their own power, and their own destiny. Rather than seeing any event as an infinitesimal blip on the screen of their lives, most of them cannot see past this one day, this one bad grade on a report card, this one betrayal by someone they thought was a friend. Adding to their confusion are too many freedoms, too many opportunities, and too little parental supervision to prevent them from sliding down a very bumpy hill. Your children may not have all the worries enumerated here, or they may have more, but they are not coasting through these teen years without daily anxiety.

Peer Pressures

Topping a teenager's list of concerns is fear of not being accepted by peers, something we will cover in greater depth in the section on dangerous misfits below. For now, keep in mind that you have no idea how much their thoughts are consumed by saying and doing what they hope will win them friends, peers who will decide their fate and under whom they will be forced to exist throughout the middle school and high school years.

Time Pressures

Today's youngster is balancing extremes – days are filled with schoolwork, late afternoons with activities, and nights with homework, phone calls, instant messages and television. Sound like a lot of fun? Not really. Most schools begin their classes earlier than your adolescent's body is able to handle smoothly. It hasn't had time to synchronize its biorhythms, and thus exhaustion overrides his or her ability to focus and concentrate for at least the first hour of the day.

Growing teen bodies need sleep in the morning and crave the night life, yet are forced to adapt to the school's schedule. As a result, teens often have difficulty with class participation, memorization, attention, note taking and tests. They also have to squeeze in time to eat breakfast and lunch, worry about being beaten up or molested if they have to go to the bathroom, and wish their stomach wasn't growling. Finally making it through the school day, they must rush to practice or meetings, usually starving, sweating or getting yelled at by a coach for the next two hours. At last they must take their wounded pride, pack it in their backpack with their homework, and hope to catch a ride home.

When they arrive home, if there is no parent to greet them, they have to make their own dinner or a snack. If a parent is home, they may find themselves starring in a repeat performance as the ne'er-do-well who once again has caused his or her parent's anger and disappointment by doing something improperly or by not doing something they should have. They are then excused to their room, where they must choose between homework and talking with their friends. When they fall into bed they promise themselves to wake early to finish assignments, but the next day's exhaustion just begs more sleep.

Stimulation Overload

The above examples may sound like an exaggeration, but they are not. In fact, in our experience they are an understatement. Our children have been marching toward burnout before they were old enough to attend school, their overachieving and conscientious parents exposing them to every possible activity offered, from sports to dance, from arts and crafts to musical instrument instruction.

Young children's toys, once meant for idle fun and mindless activity, are now geared for educational purposes with blinding, whirling lights, shrieking noises and bells, and computer screens which announce correct answers to a two-year-old. Their little brains are scrambled by too much stimulation, hours of mindless television, and spending hours sitting in car seats while they and their siblings are raced from one side of town to the other in search of more activity and more learning. They are pressured to make the grade by kindergarten to insure they will not become an embarrassment to their parents by first grade.

It is little wonder that our children are now "bored" if they have a moment to themselves. They simply don't know what to do with free time. Their parents don't know what to do either, throwing up their hands in disgust without seeing their own early input underlying their child's boredom.

It is rare if a child picks up a book for the simple pleasure of reading, or takes a walk without an iPod or a cell phone just for the simple pleasure of being outdoors, enjoying nature. The need to fill every moment with riveting excitement often leads to risktaking behavior, with the ante raised as each thrill becomes mundane. Many teenagers are addicted to stimulation; they cannot sit still, they cannot think, they cannot just *be*. They are already exhibiting the symptoms of depression, anxiety, attention deficit disorder and burnout.

Anxiety and Depression

Who is really watching your teenager? If your son or daughter has little or no motivation, has lost their sense of humor, feels as though they carry the weight of the world on their shoulders, cries or holds feelings in, is withdrawn or aggressive, please stop whatever it is you are doing and pay attention. Your child needs you. Don't expect his or her teacher to identify or fix the problem. Teachers have neither the inclination nor the time to do your job.

Our children en masse are close to the breaking point. They are unsure of who they are and what they may become. They are standing so close to the edge they often don't know whether to turn back or jump.

If you think children do not suffer from depression you may be among the majority, but you are also wrong. Not all depressions manifest as overt sadness, moodiness and crying. Many teens resort to isolation and withdrawal, some to "cutting" (self-inflicted injury). Others may obsess about their body image and try to control their environment by controlling their food intake, either by withholding nutrients through inadequate ingestion of food (anorexia) or by binge eating and then vomiting (bulimia).

Unfortunately, both anorexia and bulimia are more common than originally thought just ten years ago. These eating behaviors cannot always be controlled by the individuals displaying them; therefore, immediate steps must be taken to seek professional assistance for any child you suspect of abusing their bodies by anorexia or bulimia. Also, if your teen confides in you that they have witnessed or have knowledge of friends who manifest these behaviors, the situation is serious enough to be brought to the attention of the parents of those teenagers. This disorder can very quickly take on a life of its own with tragic and catastrophic results, leaving parents with many unanswered questions and lifelong, often unwarranted, guilt.

The sooner eating behaviors are evaluated and treated by a team of licensed clinical psychologists, physicians and psychiatrists, the better the prognosis for these young adults. Although anorexia and bulimia are more commonly found in the female gender, males are not immune from the disorder. Because of a multitude of physical, emotional and psychological factors, eating disorders are among the most difficult to treat. Often teenagers must be treated in an inpatient facility specifically designed to treat anorexia and bulimia as they learn to accept their bodies, regain normal perspective, address their underlying emotional needs, and start on the road back to health. Without intake and weight monitoring, along with intensive psychological intervention, the prognosis is guarded.

Even very young children suffer from depression. This is not something they will "grow out of." In fact, without treatment their depression will escalate. By puberty, untreated depression begins to surface as unbearable sadness or untamed aggression. If your child appears sad or withdrawn, is consistently moody and impulsive, or displays anger and aggression on a regular basis, he or she may be in need of more than love; they may

Edith, the Drama Queen?

Edith had always been a melancholy girl who seemed to view the glass of life half empty rather than half full. As she matured, she was lovingly called a "drama queen" by her family and friends, and just about everyone thought she would have a brilliant career on the stage someday. She often cried herself to sleep at night over things that seemed to be unrelated to her directly: bugs that had drowned in the swimming pool, homeless people who waited on the sides of the road with signs saying, WILL WORK FOR FOOD, and the loss of daylight as winter approached. Her moods were as changeable as the weather, and when she was happy, she was a delight. But there was a dark side to Edith, a very private side that no one saw until one day her teacher noticed the marks on Edith's arms. When asked about them, Edith made up a story about scraping herself during a fall, and the next day and the day after that she made sure she covered her arms with long-sleeved clothing, regardless of the temperature. A month later the same teacher noticed scars near Edith's wrists and brought her to the school nurse to have a look. It was then that Edith admitted to "cutting," but said she didn't know why. Her parents brought her into therapy with tremendous concern.

be in need of professional assistance. Rather than hoping your teenager is simply going through a difficult phase from which you assume they will recover, it is prudent to enlist the help of a psychologist to evaluate their thoughts and feelings in a safe and secure environment and provide treatment if necessary. For those of you who believe that you are sufficiently trained to recognize the degree of emotional suffering which your child may be experiencing, let us assure you that you can neither identify nor treat their problems without the assistance of a professional.

At first Edith did not admit to anything being wrong, but after several weeks she began "making things up" just to patronize her parents' demands for an explanation. It was several months into therapy, after she had gained a rapport with the therapist, that Edith confessed she had been sexually molested by an older teen living on the same street. He convinced her to allow him to do things which she did not want to do, but out of fear of his wrath, she allowed him to touch her. He threatened her if she told anyone, and the secret caused such anxiety that her outlet became cutting. Her depression had taken the form of turning against herself for her "participation" in something she knew was wrong.

Edith learned to forgive herself and take back her confidence and self-esteem. With the support of her counselors and parents, she reported the molestation to the authorities. Her anxieties lessened after several months of therapy, and she went on to attend a college several states away. On her winter and spring breaks, she came back to therapy for what she referred to as a "tune up." Her depression has been sufficiently managed, and although she has some down days, she has opted not to take any medication. We are glad to report that, at this writing, Edith is in a very healthy relationship with a man who has just graduated from the same college she attends.

If the problem is that you are in denial or your fear that such treatment will cost too much money, you will regret that decision to the tune of hundreds or even thousands of dollars and unnecessary heartache. It is because you love your teen that you need to recognize that you must *get* help for them when they cannot help themselves.

What could be so terrible, so life hampering, so overwhelming that your teenager cannot cope? The answer is *everything*. As we noted at the beginning, your adolescents certainly can't control their home life, for starters. If you and your spouse fight, or are divorcing; if you are a single parent with financial worries; if the nonresidential parent doesn't spend time with them or the residential parent resents them, these issues alone are reasons for depression. Then, when you add the burden of school, where grades are regarded as the indicator of worth and peers as the magical gateway to acceptance, we don't have to look much further for the roots of teenage depression.

Dangerous Misfits

A few decades ago, the worst that could happen if children were shunned by their peers was loneliness. That is barely touching the surface of what today's children must endure. If your teenage son or daughter has been deemed an outcast by peers, he or she will spend at least eight hours of each day on the fringe of school society. That's each day for the next six or seven or more years of life lived in isolation, humiliation, sadness and fear.

Who are the boys or girls who do not fit in? Anyone whom the group deems uninteresting or unpopular, for a myriad of illogical and cruel reasons, is subject to a cruel fate. If, for example, your child is fortunate enough to have been born with a high intelligence quotient, you may not know it but he or she may be downplaying their intellect to be like everyone else and fit in with their peers. Perhaps he might excel in academics, yet be sitting in a school that places high value on athletics, or she might be athletically proficient in a school in which grades are the sole determining factor of popularity. Your child might have a physical need to wear glasses or braces, might suffer from acne or greasy hair, have inferior clothing, a speech impediment or excessive body odor, or be chosen as the teacher's pet. A child may be deemed unpopular because he or she lives on the "wrong side of town," or because a parent has been in the newspaper or in jail. Popularity is like winning the teenage lottery, and most will pay any price to be in the game.

Your children are being judged by a subculture of their peers. If these "judges" deem them as misfits, your unfortunate teenagers are forced to forever stand on the periphery, as outside observers. From this position, they may be willing to do *anything* to be accepted, including using drugs or alcohol, engaging in violence and crime, or joining a dangerous gang. The need for acceptance is so powerful that it supersedes intelligence, conscience and moral values. No, your son or daughter has not lost the sense of right and wrong, but without friends they stand defenseless among their enemies. The absolute need to fit in with one's peers drives many children to behave in an irresponsible and potentially dangerous manner.

If your child is afraid to attend school, he or she may have reasons which they do not feel comfortable disclosing. Schoolyard bullies are no longer content with namecalling; they are the hunters of the weak and they prey on fear. Your child may be the target of these cowards. If your teenager is isolated, doesn't blend in, doesn't fit, he or she faces unmerciful badgering and possible emotional and physical harm.

If you are appalled by what you have just read, imagine what it must feel like to be your child. Your teenagers are not exempt from peer review. Even if they consider themselves lucky enough to be among the popular group, their initiation and continued

Asperger's Syndrome

Keith came into therapy through the court system, having been found with marijuana on school grounds. His mother informed us prior to his initial session that Keith suffered from Asperger's Syndrome, a form of autism. Unusually intelligent, Keith had managed to have some friends in the lower grades because of his popularity with other smart children his age, but as he reached puberty it was quite clear that Keith was completely lacking in social skills. Upon his arrival, he did not make eye contact with us, but rather seemed to study his environment. His parents were quick to speak for him, and unless he was asked a direct question that could be answered with a short phrase, he was unwilling to interact.

By our fifth or sixth meeting, Keith had come to look forward to his sessions, although his outward appearance had not changed much: His face was expressionless, his posture stiff, and his hands found comfort placed on his thighs at all times. When asked how long he had smoked pot, he answered simply, "I never smoked it." Astounded, we backtracked our assumptions, beginning with the school's interpretation of what constituted marijuana usage, followed by the court's confirmation. Yet, he stood firm in his denial. "I never smoked it. I only held it." He missed the shock in our faces because Asperger's Syndrome victims have difficulty "reading" people. He simply stood there in the therapy office, surrounded by two counselors and both parents, but very much alone. "I just wanted to be like everybody else," he said.

membership in the group remains conditional. They must behave in a similar manner as the majority or risk expulsion and excommunication. We are living in dangerous times, and schools are not any safer than any other public facility.

Many schools now employ police officers, referred to as "resource officers," to walk the campus, on the lookout for suspicious activity or fights. Your child is only as safe as the vicinity of the closest resource officer. We have all heard about bomb threats and gang fights, kids who bring guns to school and actually shoot people. If such incidents haven't occurred at your child's school, you aren't sufficiently prepared for when an incident does occur. It is human nature to think this won't happen to your child, but human nature doesn't wear a bulletproof vest.

Information and Protection

If you are to protect your children, you must arm yourself with information. Get involved in the school system and the PTA, meet your children's teachers and inform them of any problems such as a pending divorce or bullying on the school bus. Request that they notify you of any changes in your teen's behavior. Should you have a "gut" feeling that something is amiss, go with it – that means, take action! (We are staunch supporters of trusting our gut feelings, which, if allowed, will usually knock on the door of concealed truths.) An overworked teacher is first a human being and, as such, will make time to observe your child and be an extra set of eyes and ears. Since your son or daughter is not equipped to know how to identify a serious situation, he or she should be instructed to take *any* threat seriously and report it to the school authorities. School faculty or administration are only able to protect your child if they are alerted to a potential problem.

It goes without saying that your teenager will fear retribution if he or she snitches on bullies or reports other menaces. Although you cannot make the promise of complete confidentiality, you should tell your child that every effort will be made to handle the problem without his or her direct involvement if possible.

Your child's school should have a program of confidentiality and immunity when one child turns in another.

Jason's Problem

Jason came into therapy after asking his parents to find him someone to talk to. We were surprised at how reluctant he was to express his problems after his parents told us of his willingness to come into the office. It was very difficult for Jason to actually say aloud what he had been trying to avoid thinking about for years.

Jason had been in a physical education class in sixth grade. After an hour-long hockey game on a hot spring day, when everyone stripped down to shower, one of his teammates took a look at Jason's penis and yelled across the entire locker room, "That's the smallest thing I ever saw. You can't be two inches long."

That incident had occurred five painful years earlier, but Jason never told his parents of his humiliation, nor did he confide his "problem." And unfortunately, unlike many rumors that are quickly squashed by the next one, this embarrassing tale was told again and again by his peers. The story and description of Jason's member followed him from grade school to junior high and finally to high school. During that time, he begged off any further physical sports involvement, pretending to have a

If there is no such program in place, you can be instrumental in organizing one.

If you believe that your teenagers are unsafe in their school environment, there are several options. Private schools, while expensive, offer a smaller class membership and, therefore, more careful observation of a child who is being bullied or isolated. Enrollment in a private school means that every student is subject to and protected by that school's "bill of rights," which generally includes provisions for suspension or expulsion of any student who does not abide by the criteria of that school. This approach differs from that of a public school, where generally an infraction must have nonspecific ankle injury. His self-esteem was so low that he never had a date, never asked a single girl for her phone number, and never went to any of the school dances or the prom. In fact, not only had he never had sexual relations, he expected he never would. He certainly didn't think he was capable of intercourse, and doubted there was any chance he would father a child. His peers still made fun of him, bringing tape measurers to school and making reference to how big an arbitrary object was in relation to his penis. Once there was a roach in the classroom, and someone yelled, "Is that a roach or did Jason lose something?" The class howled, and Jason pretended not to be offended. He was good at pretending that his feelings weren't hurt; he'd had quite a bit of experience.

In therapy he could finally vent his feelings, crying over every hurt and humiliation he had encountered over the years. It was some consolation to him to finally realize that he could have relations and father children, but the stigma of size was a huge detriment. He did not want his family to know, and his confidence was kept. At this writing, Jason is finishing college, and still does not have a girlfriend.

already occurred for the child to be suspended or expelled. To be sure, however, some private schools may include among their student body children who are displaced behavior problems from public school, funded with their parents' money to get a second chance. Yet, no amount of money can buy a school's reputation, and you can be assured that if that child continues to exhibit bad behavior, he or she will be expelled from the private school as well.

Another option is parochial school or another school with a religious affiliation. As in private schools, the student body will be expected to perform both academically and socially according to the school's standards or risk being asked to leave.

Rebecca's Anxiety

Rebecca came into the office as a direct referral from her medical doctor. She had missed more than twenty days of school in the first four months, and although she had vague complaints of headaches, stomachaches, and generalized malaise, her tests were negative. During the initial intake and social history, Rebecca denied any problems at home, but as soon as the subject of school was broached, she broke down sobbing. Apparently, there were some girls in another class who "had it in" for her and punched her in the stomach as they cornered her in the girls' bathroom. One of the girls rode the bus with Rebecca and made statements to her such as, "You won't know what day it will be, but when we come to get you, there will be no place to hide."

Rebecca gave us permission to speak with her parents, as well as with school officials, identifying the accused girls by name. The school promised anonymity to Rebecca, but she remained fearful of retaliation. Within one week of Rebecca's report, all but one girl had been expelled from school and placed in an alternative school. As of this writing Rebecca remains in treatment for anxiety, and it is likely that her anxieties will continue throughout high school, and may, in fact, follow her even longer.

Homeschooling – which allows for the removal of your child from public or private schooling altogether – is another increasingly popular option. This option can *only* be successful if the parents are committed to providing the necessary time and resources to educate their children responsibly. Homeschooled students are still subjected to the guidelines mandated by your state and must successfully pass nationwide standardized tests which are prerequisites for graduation. Often children who are homeschooled have the benefit of conscientious parenting with a wealth of information and hands-on experiences in their "classroom" without walls.

Only you know what type of school you are sending your child to every day. Only you know if your child is happy there, if he or she makes and keeps friends, excels in classes, and greets the day with enthusiasm. Only you can offer your teens the best alternative regarding where they spend almost half their waking hours. Please save them if they need to be saved.

Chapter 6

Respect, Respect, Respect

We have briefly mentioned the fundamental idea of mutual respect. This topic is sufficiently important to warrant its own chapter. Without it, you will be unable to master any techniques for permanently reshaping your teenagers' behavior.

There is an old saying that "respect must be earned, not demanded." While that is true, if it is earned and still not given, as a parent you will have to take it one step further. You have already established your place in the hierarchy of the household, and therefore, by rank, you are to be respected. You do not beg or plead to be treated nicely, but because of your station in life, as the authority figure in your child's world, you are to be given respect or administer consequences until the lesson is learned. It is just that simple. No respect, no privileges.

You agree in theory, and yet you allow your teenagers to do things to the contrary. You allow them to raise their voices, talk over you, walk away in the middle of your sentences, argue and debate with you, badger you, or roll their eyes when you ask them to pay attention. Then, after you are finished speaking, you walk away with the uncertainty of whether anything you have just said has been heard and will be obeyed. We can only ask, *What is wrong with you?*

Do you not want to be respected? By not commanding respect, you are teaching your child to not only disrespect you but all authority figures. Perhaps you are still confused as to the definition of "disrespect" – namely, anything which purposefully undermines a person with either blatant objections or complete indifference, evidenced by physical distractions such as eye-rolling or other overt infractions such as walking away or arguing.

None of this disrespectful behavior is to be tolerated. *Not even one time.* If you do not gain control over your children, the disrespect they display in the privacy of their home is the rehearsal for the disrespect which will later filter down to their teachers, police officers and strangers on the street. You are not raising your teenagers in a bubble; you are raising them to matriculate into society. You owe it to the rest of us to do your job, take the harder road, and punish them each and every time they behave disrespectfully until they come to the realization that they will have to change their behavior and attitude or live a self-inflicted miserable existence.

Your child's inability to display respect outside the walls of your home will culminate in a phone call from school authorities or the police department. If a bus driver suspends your child for cursing on the bus, or for not sitting in their seat when told, you will have to take the word of the bus driver over your child, because you were not there. Unless you believe that your offspring would never utter a curse word or behave in a disrespectful manner because you have never seen any display of disrespect, you should take the word of the educator, bus driver, police officer, librarian, or neighbor. We believe in standing behind your child in many areas, but in regard to respect, he or she is either right or wrong. And since we already know that our teen is not perfect, the preponderance of evidence says that the teenager is wrong.

Discipline is not going to change behavior if it consists of spending one hour in detention hall with buddies and girlfriends, all wearing their infractions like badges of honor. Take this opportunity to enforce your own consequences, which should be far stricter than what a teacher is able to do with school policy or state restraints. If you think that your teenager's mouthiness or disrespect to a teacher is no big deal, think again. It is this disrespect that is the underpinning of every crime committed and of a careless disregard of rules, regulations and authority.

Respect does not only apply to other humans, it applies to property as well. Defacing property through graffiti or vandalism, loss of property through carelessness, or possessing property which your child does not own indicates a serious problem and should be evaluated. Suffice it to say that although you cannot be held completely accountable for the behavior of your child, every time he or she behaves disrespectfully is a reflection of you.

Chapter 7

Behavior and Consequences

*C*onsequence or *punishment*? Although there may be some who argue the distinction between these terms, we have chosen to use them interchangeably. A consequence/punishment is one of the best ways we know to gain your teenagers' attention as you redirect their behavior. The loss of a privilege or the addition of a chore will interfere with their agenda and become a small and temporary disruption. Your teens do not like to have their lives disrupted, which is why a consequence or punishment is so effective. However, a consequence is only as powerful as its application. When implemented properly it will have the desired effect of modifying behavior.

A consequence should be "pure," meaning without the contamination of parental confusion, guilt or anger. Such purity is essential to keeping order and perspective. Your adolescents, however, will view consequences in a different light, believing that these consequences represent your desire to ruin their lives by interrupting their social schedules as well as the private lives to which they believe they are entitled.

We as a society cannot let our children run amuck, devoid of respect for rules and regulations. As a parent you must do your part to protect not only your child, but your children's children, so that they can live free, harvest dreams, shoot for the stars, and hang the moon.

The Behavioral Chart

During times of heightened stress, it is normal to lose the ability to think clearly and rationally. For this reason parents must be proactive in their approach to anticipated negative behaviors from their teenagers and plan the consequences in advance in a well thought out fashion. We recommend using a behavioral chart, constructed *with* your teens, which lists your expectations with regard to their behavior, paired with a consequence for any behavior that is not acceptable.

At first glance, this type of chart (see page 54) may seem juvenile. Yet it can be quite effective with adolescents in sidestepping the volatile emotions that are bound to appear following an infraction and parental confrontation. By listing both a behavior and a consequence, in black and white, *before* an offense is

Communicating with Cindy

Cindy and her mother were very much alike – opinionated, headstrong and unwilling to back down from an argument. Constant belittling and sarcasm mixed with screaming matches and long periods of time without speaking to one another seemed a way of life for this mother and daughter. Both, however, were quick to agree that they loved each other very much, but they certainly needed some redirection in their communication skills and some help in expressing mutual respect. One day, during a particularly volatile disagreement, Cindy's mother had finally had enough, and she told her daughter, "You are grounded for the next six months. I'm taking your car away and selling it, and you are going to spend your entire school year going to therapy for talking to me this way."

When they arrived in our office, neither was speaking to the other, attempting to use us as the mediators in their conversations. It was obvious that Cindy did not believe that her mother was going to be able to enforce the punishments she had threatened during the heat of battle, but, committed, there will be less temptation later to allow your anger to overshadow your ability to be rational and fair, or to prevent undeserved self-inflicted guilt.

Besides the challenge of maintaining consistency, the main bump in the road of teaching your teenager through behavior modification is guilt – that guilt which he or she will try to place on your shoulders, and which you will likely accept if you "shoot from the hip" with your consequences. Well thought out plans, constructed by both of you, will diminish or eradicate that guilt and place the responsibility squarely where it belongs – on the shoulders of the offender.

nonetheless, she was enraged at the mere thought that her car was used as a threat. We were not pleased that "therapy" was used as a threat, since the idea of establishing a rapport with a counselor is that it should be something intimate and bonding, where trust and a desire to express feelings and work toward understanding behavior is a success, not a punishment.

Over time, both Cindy and her mother learned how to communicate with considered words rather than with purely emotional reactions, and Cindy's mother did not make threats that she did not plan to uphold. She did, however, stick to a behavior chart with its consequences, quickly modifying the dysfunctional behavior which had heretofore not responded to idle threats and screaming matches. Within six months Cindy's behavior had not only improved at home, but she had learned to be more kind and considerate when speaking with her peers. Cindy enjoyed therapy so much that she had to be persuaded to cut her sessions back, with the assurance that we would be only a telephone call away.

Sample Behavioral Chart

Here is one behavior-consequence chart. Use it as a model to make your own, but personalize it completely, including anything and everything within the parameters of your expectations.

Infractions	Consequences
Room unclean, first offense	Television off for 1 hour
Room unclean, more than once	Television off for 4 hours
Room unclean, repeatedly	No television until room is clean
Chores not done	No telephone privilege for one hour
Chores not done, repeatedly	No telephone privilege for entire evening
Late curfew, less than 15 min.	Warning for first offense
Late curfew, more than 15 min.	Grounded for Friday night
Late curfew, one hour or more	Grounded for weekend
Late curfew, repeatedly	Loss of car for weekend
Disrespect to parents	Sent to room to write two-page apology letter
Disrespect to parents, ongoing	Grounded for weekend
Disrespect to parents, ongoing	Grounded for weekend, loss of car, loss of phone

Fairness

In making your behavioral chart, strive for fairness in both your expectations and your consequences, keeping your lists age appropriate and taking into consideration your teenager's schedule. Obviously, if your son or daughter comes home from school each day by three o'clock, he or she will have more time on their hands than if they don't come home until seven, after club meetings, music lessons or football practice. Similarly, if they complete their homework in study hall, they will be less apt to be resentful of chores than if they come home with three or four hours of homework. Each chart should be individualized for your teenager with regard to their activities, level of commitment to homework and studies, and extracurricular activities. Also, this chart should be flexible enough to allow for unexpected events, emergencies, and unforeseen circumstances that may supersede activities or consequences as you see fit.

Fairness is always an area of mixed opinion, but ultimatums are dealt with less favorably than allowing your young person some control. For example, if you ask your son or daughter to clean their room, rather than saying, "Do it right now," the more fair way of presenting your request would be to say, "Clean your room sometime between Monday and Wednesday." That span of forty-eight hours is fair and allows your teen to budget time accordingly, while learning to prioritize other, more attractive activities. Resist the temptation to remind your child if he or she is not on task; personal time management is all part of the learning experience to organize and prioritize. If your teenager has a room-cleaning window of two days in which to carry out the task, that means two *complete* days. Do not mention the infraction until forty-eight hours have passed.

Reminders

Once you have given any directive, do not repeat it. You are teaching your adolescent nothing if your nagging reminders shield them from experiencing the consequences of their own distractibility or absentmindedness. It is normal to "forget" a task that is unwanted and uninteresting. If your teen anticipated a trip to Universal Studios, he or she would certainly have that event scheduled into their mental day planner. Remember, your son or daughter is neither stupid nor deaf; they are simply not eager to march to *your* drum. But again, although we respect your children's individuality, we are also reminding you that they must fit into society, which translates into following rules and

Forgetful Bob

Bob's parents worried that he would not "make it" in the real world when he graduated from high school because of his "inability to do the most simple things." They brought him into the office to be tested, concerned "that he might be retarded." Bob followed directions in the office without hesitation, having no problem remembering what was asked of him. When asked to memorize a series of words and then repeat them back at the end of the session, he also had no difficulty in performing. His parents were astounded. "He can't remember to pick up his clothes from the floor or take out the garbage. Last week we asked him to take the dog out, and three hours later, after the poor dog soiled the floor, Bob simply said he forgot," his dad explained. Bob's mom chimed in, "We ask him at least four or five times a day to empty the garbage, but he just can't remember anything. I'm just so worried about him."

From our perspective, Bob had a pretty good thing going, and he was about to get busted. He no more had a learning problem than his parents did, but he quickly recognized that he could manipulate them into believing that he was inept and inadequate, which worked to his advantage when it came time for him to take on any responsibilities. After a series of questions, regulations. In the case of an untidy room, they will now not only have to clean their rooms on your terms, but will also have the added consequence according to the behavioral chart, which will help them make a better choice next time . . . and there most certainly will be a next time.

Avoid bringing up past issues and combining them with current problems. This will escalate the ire of your teenagers and cause them to be defensive. For example, the next time your teenager's room is untidy, rather than say anything simply go to the chart,

we had determined that Bob played on a basketball team, was quite a baseball enthusiast, and had always been something of a ladies man. "How many home runs did Yogi Berra hit?" we asked. Bob answered without hesitation. He not only knew baseball stats, but football as well. "How do you do on your basketball team?" we asked. "I was voted most valuable player this year," Bob answered. As for girlfriends, we asked, "How do you take them out?" "I pick them up in my car," he answered. "Ever get lost?" we asked. "Lost?" Bob laughed out loud. "No, why would I get lost?"

It didn't take long for Bob's parents to figure out where this was heading. Bob didn't have a problem with learning things, memorizing things, and doing things, so long as they were things Bob wanted to do. Relieved and furious at the same time, Bob's parents immediately instituted our plan, which was to give Bob an instruction once and expect a job to be completed. If it was not completed within a specified time, they would administer a nonnegotiable consequence.

After that, we only had to see Bob and his family once more. Bob's game had come to a screeching halt as his parents reestablished their control through reasonable expectations and rewards or consequences.

find the consequence for repeat offenses, and administer it. Saying something such as "You never learn, do you?" will further aggravate an already trying situation.

Seriousness

Giving a consequence is serious business; you are teaching your son or daughter a life lesson. If you find this process amusing or laughable and show it in any way, your teenager will immediately pick up on your cue and not take it seriously either. Parents sometimes minimize the consequence due to their own insecurity. Don't express this insecurity! You have every right to expect to be respected and obeyed. If you minimize your teenager's decision to pay attention to a request, you have just taught them to bend the rules. They will learn nothing from your ambivalence other than your inadequate parenting skills.

Duration

We strongly advise that you do not take away any privilege or activity that is going to negatively impact your teenager's life or future, and do not issue consequences with a long shelf life. One night or, at the most, one weekend without privileges will achieve the impact you desire; anything more than that comes under the category of "cruel and unjust" punishment, as determined by your child and seconded by us.

For excessive infractions, or the same infraction repeated over and over, obviously there will be more privileges taken away and more time added. If a consequence is given for more than a night or a weekend, not only does it lose its effectiveness but your rigidity or punitive nature becomes suspect. Longer consequences do not equate with how skillfully the lesson is learned; in fact, quite the contrary. When children can never climb out of the punitive hole, they simply rebel and become more difficult to manage in direct proportion to their anger.

Lessons taught with fairness and love within the shortest time possible and with true angst that your youngster is unhappy will be successful in their results. Remember, even in the face of your anger or disappointment, your teens are still learning, and in their worst moments of disrespect and verbal assaults they are angry at themselves for having disappointed you. Although they are all dressed up in teenage clothing, they are still just children.

Don't Forget the Rewards

As well as using a behavior-consequence chart, you might also want to hang a behavior-reward chart – indicating, for example, when and how your teen will be rewarded for coming home every night for one month within curfew. We like the idea of giving a monetary or other reward for excellent effort and ability in following rules. All of us are rewarded in some manner for the things we do: We go to work, we receive a paycheck; we make a good dinner, we get compliments. Your child is no different. Although people may disagree with us, we have attracted more flies with honey than with vinegar. Translation: *If you want your teenagers to learn how to follow the rules, make their wise choices a source of reward.*

Chapter 8

You Own Their Stuff

In the previous chapter on behavioral consequences, you were encouraged to create a behavior chart, identifying an infraction and pairing it with its consequence. Still, you may be left with the common question, "How do I get my teenager to comply?" That question can be answered easily with common sense and four little words: "You own his stuff."

"You own their stuff" means that you have the ability to pull out all the stops, since your position in the family gives you any leverage needed to insure your teenagers' compliance. Think of it; not only do they reside in *your* home, they basically own nothing. You own their room, the refrigerator, the television set, the computer, and the telephone. Even if your son or daughter has a cell phone or car, if the account has your name anywhere on it, you own these items. The sooner you realize that, for the time being, the material possessions to which your child is so attached can be used for collateral, the better off you will be.

Redirecting your teenagers' behavior is serious business and cannot be achieved with whining or pleading on your part. When you begin eliminating those items to which they believe they are entitled, they will quickly feel the earth move under their feet.

Without question, food, clothing and shelter must be provided, but perhaps not in the style to which your adolescents have become accustomed. Items such as a Game Boy, iPod, computer, cell phone and television set are simply on loan, from you to them. Removing these items as a consequence of unacceptable behavior will have an immediate impact. Hopefully, the impact will be sufficient to redirect behavior. While you are compiling the list of items that are invaluable to your teenager, don't forget air time – including cell phone, Internet, My Space and instant messaging.

Stay Realistic / Stay Balanced

A little power in this domain of making consequences and withholding "stuff" goes a long way, and we don't want you to get ahead of yourself, all giddy with your plan for redirecting your teen's behavior. You may be tempted to veer from the chart and make a consequence on the spur of the moment; one which will be impossible to uphold. A parent who doles out a restriction such as "You will never see the outside of your room until you are twenty-one" will quickly come to regret the statement, usually uttered when your teenager has done something exceptionally heinous, such as causing you unbearable worry as to their whereabouts, or returning home hours after curfew, without permission.

Generally, fear of unthinkable harm is enough to push a parent into making an unreasonable and ridiculous threat such as the one above. Unfortunately, the moment the words leave your lips credibility is lost; your son or daughter does not for one moment believe that they will be sequestered to their room for the next four or five years, and so they go to bed confident that morning's light will put things into perspective.

This lack of realism and balance is not the message you want to convey! What you want your children to believe is that you are in full control of your faculties, and the way to gain credibility in their eyes is to calmly follow the chart made for exactly this reason. If you honestly do not believe you can do this convincingly, rather than allowing your emotions to speak for you, tell your teenagers that you will deal with the infraction tomorrow. At the least, this will cause them added worry, and you will not have to recant your position in the morning.

Regardless of the infraction, it is unnecessary to belabor your shock and disappointment. Your child feels bad enough, and to

Susan's Stuff

Susan's mother came into the office crying, followed by her very bored and unemotional daughter. Mom had come to her wit's end trying to get Susan to help around the house and be more pleasant to her parents and siblings. Susan rolled her eyes as her mother spoke. "She can't make me," Susan said. When we heard from her mother that her daughter's feelings of entitlement and belligerence had endured for years, Susan agreed that she was noncompliant because, "I don't feel like having anybody telling me what to do or how to act."

At our suggestion, Susan's parents agreed to come alone for the next several sessions to concentrate on their lack of basic parenting skills, as well as on their inability to rein in their daughter's dysfunctional behavior. We helped them construct a behavioral chart and explained that everything that Susan had in her possession was simply "borrowed" from them. On the behavioral chart we listed things dear to Susan, such as her iPod, her phone, her computer, and her designer purse. Then we explained that each time Susan chose noncompliance she

make him or her believe that they have become a failure in your eyes will solve nothing; rather, it will create a host of other problems that will cost you lots of money in the future as they work through their low self-worth issues on a professional's couch.

From our perspective, children are born pleasers; give them love, nurturing, encouragement, support and respect and they will try to do well by you. You could never punish a loved child more than he or she will punish themselves if you have always been fair with them. If they do mess up, and they will, please do not administer a consequence involving a milestone event. If your teenager has broken curfew for the fourth time this month and you deem it necessary to ground them for an entire weekend, would have to give up one item at a time, and that although this would cause quite an uproar in the house, the turmoil would be short-lived. Then we invited Susan into a family session to explain the new plan. She laughed at the idea that her parents actually thought they would be able to restrict her behavior, but she didn't laugh for long. By the end of the first week, Susan had laughed herself right out of everything she owned (or should we say "borrowed"). Finally, she "gave up" her resistance to her parents, but immediately insisted on getting her things back. We instructed her parents to have Susan "earn" her things back one by one, over a period of time, for consistently good behavior. Whether Susan's attitude adjusted because she had become more appreciative of her parents' time and efforts or simply because she saw a means to the end she wanted is not the point; we cannot remake people from the inside out. Some traits, however negative, will remain, albeit covertly, and that will have to be dealt with another day. For the present, Susan's family has found a way to guide their child's behavior to at least superficially become more positive.

please do not make it the weekend of their class trip, prom, or any other event that will never be repeated. Their tardiness should have no bearing on their attending the school prom, which is a rite of passage. Save the weekend grounding for the following week. They will remember this act of kindness.

Healthy Fear

Right about now we must ask, *Does your adolescent have a healthy fear of you?* If your answer is no, you have uncovered one of the reasons that your communication is not going to be taken seriously. In our opinion, all teenagers should have a healthy fear of authority figures, especially you. This does not imply that we believe in corporal punishment or physical threats, nor does it give you the green light to humiliate or otherwise embarrass your teenager in public or private. The "fear" we mention here refers to fear of unknown consequences, which, combined with your teen's imagination, should create unpleasant scenarios in their minds – scenarios of potential circumstances in which they do not want to find themselves. This "fear" propels your teenager into following your directives or having to face something potentially so awful, so unpleasant, so terrible that it is not even to be considered.

This "fear" factor was used quite effectively during the 1950s and '60s, but lost some of its luster as parents began allowing their children more of a role in their own upbringing. It is not too late to revisit what worked. Your child should not know every trick up your sleeve, and should not be able to anticipate your every move. Leaving something to the imagination goes a long way.

If you were savvy enough to have instilled a healthy fear during your child's formative years, by now he or she is fairly proficient at mastering their own negative impulses without much need of assistance from you. But, alas, in this era of permissive parenting we suspect you will join the majority of parents who will have more of a struggle. Remember to save the use of "healthy fear" for a time when you really need it, but always allow it to skulk in the background. Healthy fear is not so much a verbal threat. As with most intangible things, you will recognize healthy fear when you see it working by the look on your child's face.

"The Look" and Other Effective Tools

Effective parenting cannot be successful if your teenager does not take you seriously. If in the past he or she has mocked you, or impersonated you and your directives without correction, you have done yourself a disservice by displaying your disbelief that you are really in charge. Your offspring may be comedic and talented, heading toward a lucrative career at Second City or an Improv club, but for now the blatant disrespect must be punished. The combination of consequences, your seriousness of purpose, a healthy dose of fear, and "the look" should be more than effective. Also effective is the addition of a statement such as, "You do not want to know what will happen if you do not do as I say right now." In addition, and at the very moment of your uttering, you must give "the look."

"The look" is worth a thousand threats, and if done properly, will actually give your teenager a shiver down his or her disrespectful spine. Never use this look unless you mean business. "The look" should be given when your son takes the car without permission, when your daughter sneaks out of her window in the middle of the night, or when he or she bucks your authority in their quest to undermine you.

If "the look" and a veiled threat is not enough, and it almost always is, then you will have to impose several consequences at one time, enough to really rattle them, for you to regain your control. For example, everything they own or play with or ride in should be removed at once and returned only when they grovel their way back to you, gushing heartfelt apologies, but not before. That swift and purposeful action potentiates "the look," and once mastered achieves the goal of healthy fear.

Consistency

Owning their "stuff" gives you physical property rights to your children's possessions. That, in conjunction with referring to your behavior chart, swiftly administering a consequence, and knowing when to give "the look" – all tools which are potentiated by a healthy fear – should curtail your teens' acting out behaviors rather quickly, *provided you are consistent about consequences.* Without consistency, however, there is no chart clear enough and no stack of your child's confiscated possessions high enough to change their attitude. The only obstacle between your teenager behaving well and your teenager behaving badly is *you*.

Without consistency, you actually make every situation worse. Like any proficient detective, your child will find any weak area in you that can be broken and destroyed. He or she is equipped with special radar to hunt out your Achilles' heel and to know when you are too tired to enforce a punishment or too busy to make the punishment stick.

If you want a teenager to obey your wishes, you have to commit to parenting all the time, even when you're too tired, too sick, too overwhelmed; if not, wave the white flag of defeat and let them run wild into the streets, but not before they rob you of your pride, respect, dignity and money.

Chapter 9

Lies, Lies and Lies

All teenagers lie.

Sorry to drop that on you, but we didn't know a better way to get your attention. Lying is a distasteful subject. The act of lying is so powerful that, over the ages, it has caused personal misery and anguish, reeked havoc upon nations, provoked wars, demolished the institution of marriage, hurled victims into cyclones of despair, and splintered families. The word "lying" has such negative connotations that most people want to soften its impact by finding a more palatable one, such as "fabrication," "embellishment" or "exaggeration." Lying, by any other name, still remains repugnant, an act of deception. Whether it is overt or covert, purposeful or by omission, it strangles any possibility of arriving at the truth.

Yet, we all lie. We all commit this unforgivable offense not once, not occasionally, but often, in one manner or another, whether to avoid facing the truth or to prevent someone from being hurt by the truth. Lying is generally viewed by society as a black or white, right or wrong issue; yet, lying can also be examined in terms of gray.

Children are expected to tell the truth – we have ingrained that concept since they could understand the spoken word – and yet they are also encouraged to lie to their grandmother when they thank her for the hideous purple sweater she sent for a birthday gift. It is quite confusing for young children attempting to master the spoken and unspoken word to put together the concept of truthfulness while at the same time telling a bold-faced lie instigated by their own parent.

In general, we teach our youngsters that not everyone has good intentions and that when they become frightened or lost they can summon the assistance of a police officer. We tell them that if they go to church and listen to the preacher their burdens will be lighter. If they honor the Constitution and cast their vote, the country will be led by an honest politician. Sometimes, however, these principles fall short of the mark.

How do we teach our children about lying, when integrity and honesty are all but antiquated? By referencing the same principles that we have always believed to be true: that although not everyone is honest or truthful, telling a lie is wrong, and should be dealt with by consequences. We advise them that, regardless of evidence to the contrary, we must believe that good

Roger's Lies

Roger's parents had preached the importance of truthfulness for as long as he could remember, which is why he didn't dare tell them that he had been lying to them for the past year. Roger had told his parents that he had been earning credits at the local community college at night, while attending high school during the day. It seemed like such a little lie at first, and a good way to get out of the house to see his girlfriend. One day became a week, and then a month. His parents asked him about his courses and his grades, and he boastfully told them of his good test results. He made up course work, and even reported fictional conversations with professors. His parents were so proud of him that they told all their friends and relatives of Roger's academic ambitions and success.

After six months, Roger broke up with his girlfriend and no longer had a need to deceptively "sneak" out of the house under the guise of going to college. The more he lied, the more anxious he became, until his heart raced in his chest and he had difficulty will prevail, justice will be swift, good things come to those who wait, and the truth will set you free, because to believe otherwise is to discard hope and join in moral decline. Those liars who have publicly disregarded rules and regulations, those officials who have carelessly tossed aside our confidences and dishonored their platform, cannot be the new moral leaders to whom our young people aspire, but rather serve as a poor example of the human spirit and a worse example of a human being. In their own convoluted way, these disgraceful examples become teaching tools. We can use them as cases in point to tell our teenagers the truth and help them to integrate the disillusionment that comes with full disclosure of the fact that the world is not working as it was designed.

sleeping at night. Roger was so afraid of his parents' finding out the truth, and the disappointment he would cause them, that he actually spent five weeks in therapy anguishing over what he should do, all the while still pretending to attend night classes.

With our encouragement, Roger invited his parents into the office for a family session, and blurted out his deceptions. True to his anticipation, his parents were enraged; yet they were also relieved that he hadn't been the victim of something more sinister and serious. His mother worried that he might have been in some type of legal trouble, and his father worried that he might be grappling with being gay. Interestingly, these unfounded fears told more about his parents than they did about Roger. All Roger wanted to do was see his girlfriend, and since he was seventeen and living under strict rules, he created a way to make that happen.

It took Roger's parents less time to calm down than it did for them to reestablish trust in him, but they did admit that it took a pretty big man to "come clean."

Degrees of Lying

Because lying is so reprehensible, parents are inclined to group all lies together, but all lies do not hold the same degree of intent. Although no lie is "right," some are not as wrong as others. There are varying degrees of lying.

Lies that seek to save someone from hurt – such as not verbally admitting that you think someone looks extremely fat, when asked; or saying "she's beautiful" when a new mother offers her less than attractive baby up for inspection and expected compliments – are not the same as telling someone you are not able to meet them for dinner because you are ill, only to go out with someone else. Climbing the chart of deception, a lie about lost homework is not as bad as changing a grade on a report card; cutting school to go to the beach isn't as bad as sneaking out the window at midnight to drive a car without a license. The ultimate lie is one that lures someone into a dangerous situation for the purpose of harm.

Then there is the business of consequences for lying, and yet even that seems to have a caveat. If your child is in so much trouble that telling a lie will only put them in further danger, they must be encouraged to come forward with the truth and be offered immunity for their courage. If your child, for example, has had explicit instructions to never go into chat rooms on the Internet, and yet has not only disobeyed your directive but actually revealed identity and location and been contacted by a predator, he or she must feel safe enough to come forward for much needed assistance; if not, they might not be able to ever come forward again.

There are shades of gray mixed in with the black and white of lying. Lying, although morally wrong, can be circumstantial. However, in our experience, the majority of teenagers lie to manipulate their parents into allowing them to have what they want or to go where they want without full disclosure, or they minimize the truth to avoid punishment. These are the lies we are speaking of when we tell you that lying is wrong and is deserving of consequences.

With each deceit the path to freedom is lost, and the burden of each lie becomes the new road to moral decay.

Chapter 10

All About Manipulation

Manipulation, or the twisting of the truth with winning as its goal, is a second cousin to lying. While purposeful deceit using verbal untruths is the nuts and bolts of lying, manipulation is the creative art by which desired goals are unscrupulously attained. Both involve bending the rules, blurring the facts, omitting important data, and setting out to achieve a goal through deceitful tactics and inaccuracies.

By the age of five or six a child has already learned how to use this strategy of manipulation and is working to perfect it. One can only imagine how proficient he or she will have become in its use by the time they reach the age of puberty. For most teens, the motive for manipulation is simply to reach the desired goal, but in some teenagers, especially those with a predisposition to addictive or psychopathic behavior, manipulative behavior serves as its own reward. Some teens simply want to see if they can outsmart the authority figure.

Teenagers are master manipulators. Since childhood, they have learned through observation how their parents and siblings have maneuvered situations to achieve a predetermined gain. You are the model your children strive to become. They have been studying your ability to bend the rules as they suit you, eavesdropping on your conversations of slanted truths which they know firsthand are false, and watching your body language and listening to your intonations as your deceptions work to get you what you want. Your happiness is laced with power, and that power is what imprints mental notes on pushing limits, creative omission of facts, and smokescreening of the real issues. Congratulations.

Because of your early teachings, your teenager has aced the final examination as a master manipulator.

If you are fed up with your teenagers' manipulations, before you point the accusatory finger at them, take a good long look in the mirror. As difficult as this is to believe, it was you who inadvertently enabled them to journey down this path.

What They Learned from You

Let's revisit the days gone by, when, for instance, your adorable baby girl or boy drops a teething ring, preferring instead to grab hold of your dirty car keys. The baby is amused by the sound of the keys jingling together and intrigued by their metal ridges, so she decides to stuff them into her mouth as far as one chubby little hand can push. Horrified, you retrieve the keys before they make their way down her throat, thankful that she did not choke but still worried about the thousands of germs which made their way inside her mouth.

Your child, meanwhile, isn't worried about any of that nonsense, consumed only by her misery at having the keys taken away from her. Hair-raising screams fill the room, and nothing will distract her from wanting those filthy keys. After several frustrating minutes, embarrassed by your baby's public wailing, you make an attempt to wipe off the invisible germs, knowing the futility of this act, yet desperate to stop the crying. As you wrap her fingers around the cool metal of the keys, your child's world miraculously returns to normal. You have just taught her a valuable lesson: If I do this (cry), I get that (the keys).

Without conscious intent, the groundwork has been successfully laid and will soon be cemented by further incidents in which you give in to your child, until the art of manipulation is perfected. In its simplified form, your child digests information which translates into the mantra, "I will get what I want much faster and more successfully if I put up a fuss than if I don't."

Vanessa's Mom

Vanessa had "issues." At least that was the way her mother stated the problem when she called the office to make an appointment for her fifteen-year-old daughter. When asked to be more specific she said her daughter was "driving me crazy" by twisting the truth about "everything," both at home and at school. That didn't give us much to go by, but as the conversation pressed on, Vanessa's mother managed to leave a lasting impression. The appointment we offered her was "no good" because it interfered with "all sorts of things"; when we offered her an appointment for a week later, she said she was in dire straits and had to come in "this very day." She was told that new patients had to wait for an opening, and were not necessarily given an appointment on the day they called. In response she cited multiple relationships she'd had with doctors' offices in the past, explaining how "accommodating" they were, inferring that she was already disappointed in what she considered our "lack of empathy" for her concerns. She said she would find a

As your child matures, he or she may no longer enjoy making a visible fuss, and so begins to use language to support manipulation, weaving an intricate tapestry of premises and concepts, all created with underlying motives. Children learn which fables work and which don't. As they dissect the reasons for the failure of some stories to convince you or others, they build stronger and tighter ones, which, combined with the proper emotions, serve to achieve the desired results.

Let's take another example (which you can modify to suit your situation) to demonstrate how your children have learned the art of manipulation from you. Suppose in your family there are two children, each perceiving that the other gets more parental attention. Although you have done the best you can to dole out therapy office elsewhere and hung up. No more than five minutes had elapsed when she called back and asked if we'd had time to think about our decision, adding that her husband was taken suddenly ill and was about to be admitted for surgery. She asked us to please reconsider, for the sake of "my husband, who won't go into surgery without knowing that Vanessa will be in good hands."

As luck would have it, we did have a cancellation for later that day, and we scheduled Vanessa and her mother for a new-patient interview. Vanessa's mother was upset that we asked to speak with Vanessa alone, stating, "You'll be sorry. She won't tell you the truth; she'll just make it up as she goes along."

Vanessa entered the therapy room and within a few minutes began to feel at ease enough to give us some background information. When she spoke about her father, we interjected our good wishes that his surgery go well. Vanessa looked at us and said, "Did Mom use that surgery story? It's one of her favorites; it gets her plenty of mileage."

rewards, consequences and affection evenly, each child's skewed perceptions allows him or her to believe they have been treated unfairly. On this particular occasion it is flu season and your older child, a daughter, has come home from school with a high temperature, aches and pains.

Although your younger child, a son, was looking forward to playing on the swings in the park for the afternoon, that activity has been squashed as you become obsessed with the more pressing ordeal of taking his sister's temperature, bundling her in bed, cooking her a favorite meal, moving the television into her bedroom, and checking on her every fifteen minutes. Your younger child has little compassion for the suffering of his older sister, but is quite annoyed by your complete oblivion to *his* boredom. Determined to find a way to get your attention, he goes to bed crying. Immediately you suspect something is wrong and ask, "Are you sick?"

Before the last word has left your lips, your son, without skipping a beat, begins to hold his stomach and moan. The more he moans, the more attentive you become. Soon his little head is being propped up on pillows and a television is brought into his room as well. The smell of home-made chicken soup fills the kitchen and finds its way upstairs, while his favorite snacks are placed at his bedside. "If you aren't feeling better tomorrow," you suggest, "you and your sister will both have to stay home from school." Bingo!

Not only has your child figured out a way of diverting all the attention from his infirm sister, he has managed to secure a television set in his bedroom, have his favorite snacks brought to him, and been given the promise of no school the next day, all based on a lie. He has learned quite a bit in a short amount of time, which, when used at a later time, will again produce the same results, reaffirming his proficiency at playing this new and powerful game.

Rewards for Sickness?

Can you believe how difficult it is to parent a child? No one is blaming you for believing your child is ill when he or she tells you so; it would be remiss not to. We are simply trying to demonstrate how events, by serendipity or on purpose, can become the blueprint for manipulation.

Should you send a sick child to school so as not to support this type of parental nurturing? No, that is not the answer at all. However, unless your child is homebound with a catastrophic illness, or bedridden with a broken leg, neck or back, there is no necessity to reward him or her for being sick. As a parent you often go overboard to rescue your children from uncomfortable situations or experiences. When you cannot control these situations a part of you feels guilty as well as helpless, feeling somehow responsible for your child's suffering.

We are not suggesting that you ignore your sick children; they should certainly be put to bed and be kept home from school until they are well. No one at school is thrilled to be exposed to whatever germs your child is breeding. But if he or she is sick, they can sleep, or read, or just lie there and moan. Once they are feeling better, they can go to school and watch television afterward in the living room with a blanket thrown over them. There is no need to set up their bedroom as a makeshift infirmary. Too much attention is sometimes as detrimental as not enough. The long-term effect of overparenting during a common cold or flu is the hypochondria which follows your children into adulthood in search of an unconscious need for attention, transferred from mother to mate.

High-Stakes Manipulation

Let's explore another hypothetical example, this one of your teenager's use of manipulation for their own gain. In this example, the stakes are far more serious. The manipulation begins as "kid stuff" but escalates into something far more ominous.

Let us suppose that your daughter is invited to a party which she has a pretty good idea you won't allow her to attend. She doesn't know the host of the party, and the location is in a neighboring town. However, many of her friends will be attending and she doesn't want to be left out of the fun. She knows how you feel about her attending parties, especially at a home where you don't know the family; and besides, she knows that you have to go to bed early in order to be awake and out the door the next day for your weekly golf game or shopping date.

Since, in this hypothetical situation, she knows that you're not comfortable driving late at night, she certainly isn't going to convince you to drive her back and forth to a distant location. Certain that a request to attend the party will be denied, she sets aside the truth for a more creative version of the upcoming event.

The way your daughter views it, there are a few possible scenarios kicking around in her head. The first is a blatant lie. She can tell you that she's going to a neighborhood party, hosted by a person you like. Without hesitation, she discards that option because of the ease with which you can call the host house, where the party will not be confirmed. She will then find herself in trouble for lying and most likely be grounded before the weekend ever gets off the ground.

The more likely scenario will be more difficult to pull off, but if her performance is sufficiently convincing she may get a free pass to the party. She decides to take the chance. Without trepidation, and with direct eye contact, she converses with you enthusiastically about the upcoming party, mentioning all the friends that you know. Then she makes the story more enticing by telling you that she's arranged for transportation both ways. Next, she tells you how tiring her past week has been, playing the sympathy card which has worked so well in the past. Finally, she cinches the performance by assuring you that no one will have to worry; she has no intention of breaking curfew. To the contrary, she actually volunteers to *come home early*. Your daughter has put on a stellar performance. You have no reason to question her motives, and you are proud of her uncharacteristic concern to keep you from being inconvenienced. The "free pass" is issued.

You fall for the story hook, line and sinker, but let's dissect this performance. First there is the "hook": Your daughter casually mentions that the party is being held at a friend's house. In fact, you like all the friends in her cast of characters. The "line" is her sense of responsibility: She has already made the effort to secure transportation. The "sinker" is that she volunteers to be home before curfew, an unusual event to be sure. From our backstage vantage point, we can easily view the props and cast of characters for what they are: illusions of an overactive imagination and an underlying motive. To you, seated in the audience of this one-act play, the embellishments, omissions, exaggerations and downright deceit receive a standing ovation and curtain call.

Stopping the Show

Let's continue on with this same hypothetical example about the party, separating facts from untruths. It may be that your daughter never actually lies, especially if she really is planning on attending the party with a friend that you like. It may also be true that she has arranged transportation, so we'll give her that as well. The rest of the story, however, is a house of cards, precariously perched, and its sturdiness depends on whether or not you exercise your parental duty to assess the situation.

You have an obligation to speak with the parents hosting the party to insure they actually know about the party and that the premises will be supervised at all times. Then, you should reiterate your position on drugs and alcohol, confirming to the host's parents that you do not support underage drinking. This not only states your position clearly, it also puts the host family on notice that should any drugs or alcohol be present during the party you will take steps against them. Once you do this, you have done your parental duty, and done it well.

Now you must insure that your child will be safely transported. You not only have to know the person behind the wheel of the car, but the car itself. You will have to make sure that the person doing the driving has a valid driver's license and automobile insurance, including medical liability. You must assess the shape of the tires, including their tread, and the amount of dents and dings on the body of the car. If you do not make it your business to actually walk out to the car, shake hands with the driver, smell his or her breath, peek inside the vehicle, and pull your teenager back if the car or driver does not pass your inspection, you have done your teen a disservice; or worse, you may have just endangered her life.

Let's assume that you *always* go through the checklist we just itemized . . . except this one time, because you aren't going to be home when your daughter's ride shows up. If you *had* been around, you would have seen a young adolescent behind the wheel – someone who was unfamiliar to you – with a car that has certainly been through its share of mishaps.

This *Could* Happen to Your Teen

Let's revisit your young "adult" who wiggled her way past your intellectual radar expecting a fun night at the party. Maybe she didn't have such a good time after all; maybe before the night was over she regretted her decision and wanted to run back to the security of your family.

We all remember what it was like to be a teenager, when occasionally, for at least a few hours, we found ourselves free from the constraints of parental interference, without rules and regulations, feeling omnipotent and all grown up. It felt good. In fact it felt powerful, like nothing in the world could ruin such a night. We also remember what happened when a group of unsupervised teenagers got together, and just how quickly things could get out of hand.

For the sake of a dramatic example, let's assume that the party your daughter manipulated you into approving her attending had no adult present – that the host's parents were away visiting a sick relative, confident that their son would be responsible enough to follow the directives they issued prior to leaving. Let's also assume these parents were not irresponsible or negligent, but believed their teenager would respect their rules because he always had.

The teenage host may have had every intention of following his parents' wishes, almost to the letter. Almost. He knew he wasn't allowed to invite company to the house while his parents were gone, but he didn't think that having "a few close friends" over to watch a movie was really like having company; surely his parents didn't mean *that*!

So, that is just what this teenager did – rented a couple of movies, stocked the refrigerator with pizza rolls and soda, and couldn't wait to host the evening. The young host felt so adult. In fact, he felt pretty lucky. Too bad his friends squealed a little about the house being unsupervised. Not that these friends *meant to*, but that sort of news is just too difficult to keep quiet. Unbeknownst to the teen host, the rumor spread like wildfire throughout the school campus, one person telling another, until nothing was more important than planning to go to "the party."

By the time it was dark, the crowd began arriving. Headlights spilled over the neighboring lawns as vehicles carrying as many passengers as could fit into them parked two abreast. Before the "lucky" teen knew what hit him, people he had never even met were swarming through the door, some carrying beer, others smoking cigarettes. The smell of marijuana permeated every room in the house, clinging to the furniture like an old doily. This was going to be a great party, one to remember, hosted by just about the luckiest kid there ever was.

In such a case, it would not be "cool" to send these people packing, even if the host thought about it; and truth be known, he was so outnumbered he couldn't have controlled the scene anyway. He tried to think of what to do next. He remembered to lock his parents' bedroom door, where the jewelry box sat in plain view, but not before a couple stumbled from the tousled bed. It was going to be a very long night.

This teenager's parents didn't smoke, nor did they allow smoking in the house; yet, lit cigarettes fell out of makeshift ashtrays, burning holes in the carpet. In one corner guys were shaking cans of beer, spraying the contents at each other, as well as the furniture. Seeing all this, the host began to panic, realizing that he had completely lost the ability to control his own house. The "luckiest teen in town" was beginning to feel very unlucky.

Just when he thought things couldn't get much worse, carloads of scantily dressed girls appeared, ready to party. Within a short time, discarded condom wrappers floated on beer-soaked linoleum in a sea of sordid contamination. Jell-O shots came from a cooler, and shrieks of delight filled the house and back porch.

Meanwhile, your daughter, the story's main character, who got to attend the party through her brilliant adaptation of the role a kid who could do no wrong, finds herself pretty popular at this party; in fact, people just can't stop giving her things. The first thing she gets is a can of beer; soon after, compliments of her peers, a newly rolled joint. If you know anything about teenagers, you know that she would rather cut off an arm than say, no thanks. And so, she not only takes the offered "gifts," but imbibes them.

The buddy/friend, otherwise known as "the ride home," decides to leave for a while with a well-intoxicated partner, and doesn't make it back. Your teenager is clearly out of her league and on her own, without a backup plan. She certainly isn't going to call you; that's like diving head first into a cement pond. How is she supposed to bring you to this place filled with everything you have preached against? And besides, she has no idea where she is. She doesn't have long to worry, though, as she hears the wail of police sirens coming up the street!

Suddenly, all the "cool" partygoers don't look so cool as they jump out of open windows and doors, landing in the bushes below, running to escape. Your teen runs with them, hoping to find the main road to town.

The police call the host's parents while this unhappy teenager tries to vacuum cigarette butts and joints from the floor.

It won't be long before Mom and Dad come home. Obviously, luck has run out!

As for your manipulative teen, she finally finds a main road into town and hitches a ride. The driver, an older man, keeps glancing at your child as if contemplating taking her somewhere other than town as he mumbles incoherently. He keeps picking up the flask beside him, nervously gulping down more liquor. The drunken stranger offers your teen a couple of swigs too, which she takes out of fear. Then, too drunk to do much else, the driver drops your daughter about four miles from town. From there, she walks the rest of the way through a teeming rainstorm, arriving hours late and freezing cold. She was never so happy to see her house and, more than that, is ecstatic to see the lights out. No one has waited up for her. She sneaks into the house, peels off her clothing, and falls into bed just as the sun is beginning to rise.

You didn't think twice about going to bed before your daughter came home, what with her new sense of responsibility and all. Too bad. If you had, you would have known she wasn't even close to making her curfew. You would have been shocked to see her appearance, too: crumbled and slovenly, smelling of weed and liquor. You never thought your adolescent would disappoint you like this, and in fact, it appears she didn't. How could she, when you will never know the real story?

When you looked in on her the next morning, seeing her all flushed with sleep and innocence, you never knew how close she came to never coming home again.

Naiveté Is Deadly

If you think none of the examples above apply to you so far, think again. Your teenagers are going to manipulate you, whether you find out about it or not. To believe they were raised to know better, that they would never dupe you in this manner, that you and your teen have an open and honest relationship, is to live in

Family Dilemma

Jodi came into counseling with her entire family, including two parents and three siblings. Jodi was the youngest of the group, having just celebrated her twelfth birthday. It seemed that Jodi liked to stir the pot and cause turmoil among the family members, often by telling stories that would put her siblings in a poor light with her parents, allowing her to shine as the lone responsible family member. The latest in her series of stories was that her middle sister, Sandy, had been missing from her bed the night before, and that she (Jodi) "didn't want to tell because that would make me a tattle tale." She explained to her mom that, after thinking about her secret, she had decided to come forward because she had seen a man lurking about the yard just a few days before, and she "didn't know if Sandy snuck out of her window to meet a guy, or if there was a robber or mugger watching the house."

Mom and Dad could not believe their middle daughter would do such a thing, but Jodi told the story in such detail, even noting how the moonlight cast light on the plants, that

denial. For any teenager, there is a direct line of focus to the goal, and the goal will be attained one way or another.

You don't have to remain completely in the dark when it comes to identifying manipulation. For example, your teenagers have certain characteristics that uniquely belong to them – including the manner in which they sit or stand, walk or talk, the way they hold their head or blink their eyes – behaviors which you might not observe overtly, but subconsciously will recognize when absent.

If your teenager is relaying a story to you, there should be an organized order to that story – in other words, a beginning, middle and ending. Often, during a manipulation, your son or they felt sure she was telling the truth. That didn't sit very well with Sandy, eliciting enormous anger in her, which turned into chaos for the entire night, during which time Jodi did not back down from her tale.

After speaking with the parents in private and documenting the particulars about the alleged incident, we spoke with Jodi and asked her to tell the story, covertly comparing her story to the documented notes. They were identical. Then we asked her to retell the story, this time interrupting her at every second or third sentence to ask a question or insert an opinion. By the time we had interrupted her four or five times, we could see she was becoming agitated, losing her place in the story, and then attempting to start at the beginning each time. We asked that she begin where she left off rather than retell the entire story, and her demeanor became one of frustration and anger. She crossed her arms, pursed her lips, turned her face to the wall, and finally refused to talk to us, as her story began disintegrating. She did not appreciate being caught as the culprit rather than the savior.

daughter will speak faster than normal or, conversely, hesitate quite a bit as they weigh and measure each response. They may have difficulty making eye contact, or shift weight from leg to leg, shake a foot, or "drum" the table with their fingers. These diversionary tactics are actually assisting them as they invent the details of the story, taking their cues from your verbal and nonverbal reactions.

A technique we advise is to interrupt your teenager's train of thought as they tell the story, asking questions and keeping them off balance. They will not appreciate these interruptions, but if the story is accurate, they shouldn't have much trouble getting back on track. However, if the story begins to fall apart with your interrogation, you have punched a hole in their manipulative consciousness and eroded a shaky performance.

If this seems like an awful lot of effort just to prove your child wrong, it is, but is there a safer alternative? When you consistently oversee your teenager's schedule, if you ask reasonable questions and expect reasonable responses, if you evaluate and observe their friends and their whereabouts, it won't be long before your son or daughter gets the idea that they are at the end of a losing battle. That's good. If you're looking to score points with your teen, it won't be on this subject, but you can make up for it with unconditional love, which cannot be scored or measured.

Chapter 11
Socialization and Safety

The call to independence is so strong that most teenagers will become oppositional, defiant, stubborn and rebellious at the first perception that their thoughts and actions are constrained by a parent or other authority figure. Clearly they are not equipped to handle unexpected situations, as we have seen in the examples cited in the last chapter, yet they need socialization in order to successfully achieve this milestone of responsibility.

Adult Means Adult

Whether indoors or out, the safest place for any teenager is under the supervision of an adult, and by adult, we do not mean someone who has reached the legal age of eighteen or twenty-one. We mean an experienced, wise, savvy adult who no longer has the need to be "cool" or to "buddy up" to your child. We are talking with caution about a parent, teacher, coach, scout leader or clergy member who is responsible. We are speaking of someone who does not fall for lies and manipulations, and who can take control of heated emotions and volatility capably and quickly. If you do not know an adult who has the above qualifications, then do not leave your teen.

Leaders and Followers

Organized group activities are excellent places for teens to gather, with an emphasis on a team sport, or a meeting place arranged for studying. In clubs and extracurricular activities, peers with like interests will help each other achieve a sense of positive self-worth by recognizing their own qualities in the attributes of others. As participants, teenagers will learn to be as good followers as they are leaders, recognizing that both positions are vital to progress and success. Not every child has leadership qualities and, as much as it might make you happy to see your child's name in lights, the majority of teens lack these skills. The follower role is probably just fine with your son or daughter until you muddy the confidence waters by exuding disappointment as you push them toward the forefront. Your teen does not need this pressure from you; you had your chance to be a teenager, and whether you excelled or you stood back, you should not expect to live vicariously through your offspring.

This point is so important that we must stress it for those of you who merely scanned the last paragraph. Your teenagers are individuals with their own set of strengths and weaknesses; they cannot be something they are not, regardless of how much you push them. Being in a group in a position of nonleadership

Left Alone

Dustin showed up at the office with his father after a rather harrowing event that had occurred the night before. Mr. L., a single father, decided to go to a movie with his new woman friend after dropping his son off at the mall. Dustin didn't have shopping plans, but at sixteen he had plenty of friends who would be there and was sure he could find a ride home with one of them.

The mall closed at 9:00 P.M., three hours after he'd left his father, and Dustin could not secure a ride home. His father didn't answer his cell phone, which he had turned off prior to entering the movie theatre and forgot to turn back on. Since the mall was about seven miles from his home and he didn't want to get his dad in trouble by calling his mom, Dustin made the decision to "wait it out," figuring his father would miss him at some point and come to find him.

provides them with an opportunity to learn to work with others, accept constructive criticism, and contribute their ideas to the group as a team member. Most of all, they will be recognized as an integral part of the group with contributions to make that are both important and worthy. Leaders are not necessarily any more intelligent than followers; their strengths lie in their ability to see the big picture and delegate to the group jobs to achieve their plan. But they do not always possess the ability to persevere and follow through on their ideas. Often, if a project is to get off the ground, it is the steadfast followers who are responsible. Allow your teens to follow, if that is what best suits them.

Safety at the Mall?

There are public places where teens gather which give the appearance of supervision, but in actuality are poorly supervised, if at all. Shopping malls are a favorite with both teens and parents

He was a lone target sitting there on the curb in the dark, long after all the cars had left the parking lot, and he began to panic as he saw a group of older boys walking toward him pointing and laughing. One of them said, "Let's get him," and they all began running for him. Grabbing him, they punched him in the stomach and kicked him when he fell to the ground. Dustin yelled, but knew it was useless; no one was around to help him. He admitted thinking, "I'm going to die," when suddenly the group scattered, and the blinking yellow light of a security van shone on his beaten face. The guard called for police and an ambulance. Except for some pretty sore bones and some cuts and bruises, Dustin was physically all right. Psychologically, the trauma had caused tremendous fear and anxiety which stayed with him for quite a while.

alike. In fact, a steady line of cars drop off teenagers as young as twelve or thirteen to meet up with their friends, shop with their parents' charge cards, and stare at their own reflections in shop windows. These teenagers enjoy strolling back and forth among the shoppers, strutting in their outfits, seeking out friends, and behaving more adult-like than their wardrobe supports. Adults are thankful for the reprieve of a few hours without their teens, who are with their friends in a seemingly safe and confined area.

The mall is not your private babysitting club. Regardless of what you think, your teenage son or daughter may not be as safe as you want to believe. Because the mall employs security guards does not mean they will be significantly useful in an

Passing Inspection

Your teenager should "pass inspection" each and every time he or she leaves the house. Young girls should be able to bend over without revealing their undergarments, and show more cloth than skin. If you think your daughter is dressed appropriately, ask her to do the "touchdown signal" by raising her arms high into the air. If her shirt rises high above her midsection, or her skirt reveals anything it shouldn't, her outfit is unfit for public display.

Young men as well should be inspected prior to leaving the house, assuring that their pants are anchored at the waist by either a belt or button and zipper in the appropriate waist size. Oversized, baggy pants, "styled" to fall well below the waist, exposing areas that are meant to be covered, are inappropriate. If you aren't sufficiently repulsed by the exhibition of private areas exposed publicly, perhaps we can appeal to your concern for your teen's safety; pants hanging below the hips and unlaced sneakers make it difficult, if not impossible, to run from danger.

The idea behind teens' fashion statements is to attract attention, but the attention they attract may be not that of their emergency. In case you haven't noticed, most security guards are retired from something else; often they are either old and frail or obese and flat-footed. This is not to say that all security guards are unfit; it is to say that most of them do not look like they are capable of breaking up a brawl or wrestling down a mugger. In fact, many of them do not carry weapons, other than a telephone and walkie-talkie. In the same amount of time the security guard can telephone for help, your child may have already dialed 911 on a cell phone.

If you do decide to drop off your teens at a shopping center, advise them to put both an emergency phone number and your phone number on speed dial. If they have come to the mall

peers but of grown men who are erotically stimulated by the sight of young bodies.

Especially in single-parent households, girls can often manipulate their unwary fathers by calling them old-fashioned. They may imply that they might not want to spend much time with him if this is what they have to look forward to. Unfortunately, many fathers fall for the threat, allowing their daughter to blackmail them into submission.

Parenting is not a personality contest, where the nicest parent wins. All of you know what your children look appropriate in, and they should not be allowed outside your home without being properly attired.

This might be a good time to remind parents, especially you mothers of teenagers, that you have had your chance at flaunting inappropriate clothing. Now that you are someone's parent, you should dress age appropriately. Your child is less than thrilled when their friends talk about how "hot" you are. Button up and loosen up for the sake of your child.

with a friend and there is a threat of trouble – for instance, a group of ruffians who are harassing them – they should have been previously instructed not to leave the shopping center by themselves without an adult or police officer present. If they call you, you must drop everything and go directly to your teenager. If there is a threat of trouble, call the police and ask them to meet your son or daughter at the shopping center and stay with them until you arrive. Even in the daylight hours, heinous crimes are committed, ranging from theft to assault. A lesser attempted crime, but still within the range of things to be alert to, is carjacking. Explain to your teenager that if they feel they are being followed, or that a suspicious car is parked next to theirs, they are to go directly back into the safety of the store and call for assistance.

They should also be instructed to never enter a public bathroom without someone going with them, or at least without a crowd of people frequenting the bathroom at the same time. There really is safety in numbers, and your teenager does not automatically know this. You learned it from your parents; now it is time to pass it forward.

Whose Money Are They Spending?

Now that we have identified some of the potential dangers that lurk in shopping centers, we can pause and ponder just what these adolescents are doing there in the first place. Many of them actually appear to be shopping, which broaches the question, do they have jobs? Are they shopping with their own money? Can they be expected to use good judgment when they make a clothing purchase? The answer, generally, is that they are there shopping with Mom's or Dad's charge card, making purchases of clothing and shoes without the guidance (they would call it "interference") of their parents, who likely would not agree with their choice of clothing fit or style. Incredibly, their parents are

Samantha's Close Call

Samantha couldn't believe she was out of summer school and going to spend an entire day with her friends at the beach. They chose their spot in the sand, spread out their towels, lathered their bodies with sunscreen and cranked up the radio. Because she was menstruating, while the other kids frolicked in the ocean, Samantha preferred to hang out on the shore. After a while she took her purse and went up to the bathroom. Although it was out of the way and fairly hidden by the dunes, there was no actual door on the entryway, so Samantha didn't give much thought to being cautious. Without warning, her sixth sense made her turn around just as a scruffy-looking man entered the women's bathhouse. His hand was open in such a way that Samantha thought that he was going to try to cover her mouth. She screamed, but her friends didn't hear her from the ocean. Luckily, a couple in the vicinity came rushing to her aid. The man ran, and Samantha learned a valuable lesson in what could have been a very tragic end to summer vacation.

either too lazy, too busy, or too trusting when it comes to handing over a charge card, which at the minimum can be irresponsibly used, and at the most can be easily stolen.

We do not believe that any child should purchase their own clothing until they out of high school. This is not to say that they must shop with their parents at their side, which is highly humiliating for them. But if you venture in one direction and your child, pretending not to know you, ventures in another, he or she can choose clothing and request that the store put it on hold for an hour. Most stores, anticipating a future sale, are more than happy to accommodate this request. You can then look at the clothing before approving its purchase.

About Credit Card Use

If your teenager is given a charge card, either as a cardholder under you, or in their own name (and please note that we do not support this at all), they must be told in no uncertain terms about credit card theft, identity theft and the like. It is not beyond your parenting scope to ask to see their actual card on request, just to make sure it has not been lost or stolen.

Some parents think that giving a credit card to a teenager is going to make the teen more responsible with money. In response to that notion we ask, do you think that most adults are managing their money more responsibly because they possess a credit card? We are in favor of your giving your teenager weekly money and helping them to budget dollars they actually have, not magical dollars that reside in a shiny plastic card.

Safety Elsewhere?

Now that we have managed to put a damper on carefree evenings at the local mall, let's talk about other places where teenagers congregate and how safe they really are.

Ranking in order of greatest safety, a place of worship is probably first. Here youth groups with a religious base hold entertaining and exciting meetings, excursions and dances. If you happen to be a member of a particular denomination, you might find out what activities are offered for teens.

Organized after-school activities ranging from athletics to art and drama offer something for everyone. These clubs are geared toward expanding your teenagers' horizons as they dabble in various interests and activities, liking some and disliking others. Keep in mind that although these clubs are supervised by a teacher or other adult, there is no guarantee that your child is completely safe in them. Until scanning machines such as are used in airports and courthouses find their way into schools and other meeting places, anyone can hide a weapon such as a gun or knife underneath clothing or inside a backpack. Sadly, we have to keep safety paramount in our minds; the world has become a place of uncertainty, and even the threat of fights or gang violence is always a possibility.

If at all possible, drop your teenagers off and pick them up. Arrive early so they aren't waiting in a dark parking lot unsupervised. Most caring teachers and coaches would not leave a teenager

Socialization and College Prep

We support the position that teens don't have to finish every single thing they start, as some parents believe. If your son or daughter joins the swim team, for example, and then realizes they simply aren't buoyant, it is torturous to force them to finish out the year. Let them try their hand at a variety of things, until they find their niche.

As an added plus, colleges are looking at the *number* of interests your teenager displays, and that is often evaluated by examining the lists of clubs in which your son or daughter has participated. If you are a novice at applying to schools of higher education, we should tell you now that you can prepare for college prerequisites during your teenager's early high school years by asking guidance counselors for their input and by seeking out books at local bookstores and libraries. You can also ask for an admissions package from colleges and universities either by mail or online.

Most colleges are no longer purely interested in academic performance; they also look at factors such as national test scores, religious and club affiliations and community service. If your son or daughter does not have much evidence to show that they a well-rounded human being, they will have a difficult time competing against other kids their age. (For more about college prep see Chapter 15, "Academic Needs.")

unattended until their ride appears, but they cannot be expected to take time out from their busy schedules to babysit your teen. Arrange a time and meeting place that is not isolated, and have your adolescent call you if there are any changes in plans.

Skateboard parks and libraries are also places where teens like to congregate. If you are fortunate enough to live by the beach, there are public, supervised beaches for water and land activities; if you live in the mountains there are snow activities as well as hiking and cross-country skiing. City dwellers have a myriad of museums and parks available. Your teens should be allowed to venture out, to spread their wings and act responsibly. If they are unable to do that, perhaps they are not socially or emotionally mature enough to be left alone. Don't fret, children mature at different ages and stages. If you feel your teens are not making good decisions, keep them on a shorter leash until they mature toward semi-independence.

Support Their Socialization

While most parents have their teenagers scheduled into over-drive, there are some parents who feel quite burdened by their adolescent's desire to join an after-school club or participate in drama or baseball. They feel stressed by the enormity of their own lives and discourage their teen from anything other than what is absolutely necessary. These young people are not gaining the advantage of making friends with like interests, or of boosting their level of confidence as they achieve success in their chosen areas of interest.

We know you are tired. We are all tired. It is a huge interruption in a day to have to drop everything to carpool your teenager to and from activities which may seem unnecessary to you. But, if you want your son or daughter to be well-rounded, increase their self-worth, and gain valuable skills, you will just have to make the time. Every hour you spend getting your teen to where they have to go is a deposit in their emotional bank account. If there are few deposits, there will be little to withdraw.

Know Where They Are

We cannot stress enough the importance of knowing the where-abouts of your teenagers at all times. If your son or daughter does not come home by curfew, you should be concerned. If more than a reasonable time has elapsed without word from your teen, and they are not answering their telephone, you should notify the authorities. For this purpose, you should have a recent photograph of your child and a photograph of the car they drive, with a license plate number and registration, handy at a moment's notice. Always notice what your teen wears to school and what they wear on a date or outing; their attire may be crucial in locating them. If your teenager goes missing, an AMBER Alert will be placed on both radio and television giving a description of them, as well as a photograph.

Do not be embarrassed to notify the authorities, because waiting too long is exactly that, *waiting too long!* If your child returns home without incident and has been excessively late because of a careless disregard of your curfew, he or she may be surprised to find a police officer waiting on the other side of the front door and quite mortified to find that their face has been nationally televised. It is a lesson they won't soon forget.

Chapter 12

Privacy . . . or Not?

The only way to protect your teenagers from harm is to know what harm they may be dealing with. If you are waiting for your son or daughter to come to you with a problem, you are waiting too long to help with resolution. Most adolescents will try to work a problem out by themselves, often digging the hole deeper and deeper until they are nearly buried beneath an avalanche of trouble.

If you want to know what is going on with your teenagers, take off your blinders, polish your decoder ring, pay attention to everything they say, and more importantly, everything they don't say. You will have to sharpen your sleuthing skills as you piece together their daily activities clue by clue, skulk around corners, pick scrunched-up notes from the garbage, use your sense of smell to distinguish odors, and become proficient at noticing even subtle changes in their behavior.

As your teens become more influenced by peer pressure and more enthusiastic about events that lure them from familial teachings, they will become more careless with their words and actions. Although most of us hold the right to privacy in high esteem, raising a teenager is the exception to that right. Nothing they do or say, nowhere they go, and no one they go with, should be their own business. You should not have to hide from your son or daughter the fact that you will be snooping around to oversee their life. They won't like it, nor would any of us like someone meddling into our affairs, but unfortunately, because they are likely to make decisions that are wrong and can affect their life adversely, their every action is going to be up for scrutiny. Spying, snooping, questioning, and decoding on your part is the only way to get your teen back on track.

Possession is nine-tenths of the law; therefore, anything that is found, dropped, hidden or discarded in your residence belongs to *you*. If you find a handwritten note in your daughter's backpack; a computer-generated letter stuffed in the back of your son's desk drawer; messages your daughter has posted on her MySpace site, or any suspicious material possession, you have the right to question it, confiscate it, and destroy it.

The Real Issue

Mr. and Mrs. Y. had major concerns about their son Mitchell's increasing agitation and irritability, as well as his plummeting grades at school. Almost a senior, Mitchell hadn't bothered to fill out any of his college applications and had already missed the date for early admission. The teenager slouched in his chair, answering our questions amid his yawns, looking very much like a young man in need of sleep. His answers were based on the first thing that popped into his head rather a real attempt to convey information. In other words, it was quite clear that there was little effort being applied in school, at home, or in his initial evaluation.

We asked Mitchell to step out of the room and questioned his parents about the possibility that their son might be doing some type of drugs; they were quick to answer in unison, "No!" Treading lightly, we completed the interview and then suggested that Mitchell undergo drug testing the next day at the local laboratory. He immediately became defensive, which was fairly conclusive evidence that something was amiss. His parents reluctantly agreed to take him for testing, "just to put the issue to rest." That night, with the seed of suspicion planted in their brains, they checked Mitchell's car after he was asleep. They found drug paraphernalia as well as a small plastic bag of marijuana.

We believe it is better to warn your teen, up front, that you will be vigilant in your observations. The opposing argument is that telling them means they will not bring incriminating evidence home. That is a chance you take. But generally, between peer rumors, handwritten evidence, overheard phone calls and your teenager's surly mood, you will know when they are experiencing problems.

Problems, Minor and Serious

Many teen problems have to do with socialization: with exposing feelings to a member of the opposite sex and having these feelings minimized or not reciprocated or with being the last person picked for the team.

Teenagers may experience school problems, such as being caught cheating on a test or being held accountable for defacing school property. Perhaps a confrontative verbal exchange between your teen and a teacher resulted in the student being assigned to detention. Those problems, while upsetting to your child, are not necessarily the problems that can alter their life.

We are concerned about the more potentially dangerous and disruptive problems, such as drinking or drugs; underage and unprotected sex; the discovery of a sexually transmitted disease; depressed or angry thoughts; obsession with body image and perceptual distortion that causes a thin teenager to believe he or she is overweight; feelings of not fitting in with peers; preoccupation with violent thoughts and suicidal ideas. All of these are serious issues not only for your teenager but for the school, the town, and ultimately society if they are not identified, addressed and resolved. Minor difficulties may be handled by a parent, but generally, for problems of this magnitude to reach resolution, it is best to have your son or daughter evaluated by a professional, such as a clinical psychologist, to determine whether your concerns are simply part of a passing phase or are rooted in a much deeper part of your teenager's psyche. There is no shame in seeking professional help; the shame is in denial.

No Privacy in Computer Matters

With the advent of technology comes a double-edged sword. On one hand, information on any subject can be researched in moments; on the other hand, the computer is an open window into your child's identity. In the wrong hands, your teenagers are vulnerable to a phantom on the other end of the computer screen, a fictitious character conversing with them in a chat room, and a potential predator viewing their photographs and personal information on MySpace.

While there is always new information about strategies for monitoring the activity on your computer, such as reviewing history and using time and website blocks, there is no point in listing them here. By the time this book is in print, innovative solutions may have been discovered to keep your personal information secure and your children safe from Internet predators. However, you should be aware that these predators do exist, and they exist in alarming numbers. They are trying to lure your children by unscrupulous methods to meet them and engage in sexual acts both in person and by webcam. Teenagers are kidnapped and sold as sex slaves even in these times; by the time you know they are missing, they have already been transported to other locations and other countries.

The best way to have your child obey the rules of the computer is to have the computer in plain sight all the time. This means the computer should be locked until you are home and able to oversee their activities on the Internet. If you walk by and your teenager either minimizes or closes the screen, you can be sure the material they were just observing or writing was inappropriate; check the history. If your teen has convinced you that the pornographic sites they visited, which you discovered by checking their reference history, were simply cookies or pop-up advertisements, we have a bridge to sell you. These sights *do not* pop up unless someone in your household has left a trail of pornographic interests; we bet your teenager wishes they hadn't.

We are not big fans of laptop computers for young adults for the reasons cited above. If the computer can be moved to a private location, you do not know what is being typed. Your teenagers should not have any passwords that are exclusive to them. If they have passwords, you should know it. For example, it might interest you to know that teenagers are posting sexually suggestive, provocative photographs of themselves and their friends for the world to see. They may believe that only those who are allowed to visit their sight will view these photographs, but Internet predators are adept at seeking out MySpace sites as well as chat rooms looking for their targets.

Carlie's Serious Mistakes

Carlie had had a weight problem since she was in diapers. No matter how hard she worked at exercise and proper nutrition, she had inherited her mother's genes. It was painful for her to stand on the fringes of popularity, well-liked because of her friendliness and bubbly personality but not well-liked enough to be asked out on a date.

For Carlie, the Internet chat rooms became a source of solace and companionship; there she could pretend that she was just like everyone else, and there was no shortage of guys chatting with her. One particular guy represented himself as being seventeen, one year older than she, and living one hundred miles away. Because Carlie didn't expect to ever meet him face to face, she confided in him that she had never had a boyfriend and had never experienced a sexual relationship. Much to her surprise, her chat-room buddy began confessing his feelings for her, which quickly became "love." He said he wanted to send her flowers and asked for her home address, which she supplied.

It might also interest you to know you will find out more information about your adolescents and their friends from one or two minutes on MySpace than you knew in the past year. You will hear details of the drunken party they attended, who was caught rolling a joint, and who is sexually promiscuous with whom. As much as you would just as soon *not* know this information, you must know it; it is the only link between what your child reveals and what you discover.

Face Your Fears

How is your son or daughter going to react to your snooping? *Not very well.* They will try to inflict guilt, stating their disappointment in your lack of trust in them, as well as your shameless

Instead of flowers, he showed up in person at her house a few days later and met her at her door. Because of what she had confided, he already knew that both her parents worked and that she was home alone for at least three hours. Seeing him for the first time, Carlie was shocked at the deception. The man was not seventeen, but middle-aged and balding, with a dirtiness about him that repulsed her. At first he tried to sweet-talk his way inside, but finally barged in without permission, catching her off guard. He began peeling off his clothing as he chased her through the living room, but because he did not know the layout of her house, she escaped through a side entrance out to the street. When he fled, Carlie enlisted the help of a neighbor, who chased the man's car until the police caught up with him and arrested him for lewd and lascivious behavior and attempted sexual assault of a minor.

Carlie entered therapy for emotional support, since she would have to face her attacker in court in the near future.

disrespect of their right to privacy. This is manipulation. If you didn't recognize it, you might consider revisiting Chapter 10, where we discussed manipulation in great detail.

Some of you probably don't want to upset your teenagers, afraid of the ensuing confrontation and agitation that you are about to unleash. If your child is agitated, it is only because they have been caught doing something wrong. The fact that you don't like confrontation and try to avoid problems at all cost is a big problem for *you*, because we are going to insist that you face your fears head on, and confront, confront, confront!

Alcohol, Drugs and Privacy

Because you believe that all teenagers are going to experiment with alcohol, you might be inclined to look away when you suspect your teenager of raiding the liquor cabinet; this is wrong! Most teenagers will experiment with drinking, some minimally and others to excess, but none of them should be allowed to drink with your permission unless they are of legal age to do so. Parents mistakenly believe that since their offspring will drink (or so they assume), it would be better to allow them and their friends to drink at home under the watchful eye of the parent. This is ridiculous, not to mention against the law. If that is your attitude, why not just pour the kids a few stiff ones and let them have a ball? If you are sending the message that you do not want your teenager to drink, why on earth are you going to condone it right under your nose?

We recommend that you make it difficult for your adolescents to have access to alcohol, that you talk to them about the clear directive that absolutely no drinking will be tolerated, and that you punish them at the first indication that your directive was not followed. Serious drinking problems have their underpinnings in the family liquor cabinet. If your teenager has a drink, their already faulty judgment will only become more impaired.

There is no value to alcohol, and nothing positive will come from allowing your son or daughter to break the law.

Parents seem to have more of a handle on the seriousness of drugs than they do on drinking. Make no mistake; both are substances that impair judgment, and both are against the law if your teen is underage. The distinction is made because the law states very clearly that the use of street drugs is a punishable offense. In any event, you must be on the watch for drugs – those purchased illegally on the street, as well as stolen prescription drugs. Please remember that if a drug that has been prescribed for you is ingested without your knowledge by your teenager, that act is to be considered stealing. Along the same line, if that prescription drug is then given or sold to a friend, that is considered drug trafficking. It really drives the point home when you label it.

If you smell alcohol on your teenager's breath, it doesn't take a genius to ascertain that they have been drinking. If you see the makings of a joint – a bag of marijuana, a pipe, rolling paper or other paraphernalia – you can put two and two together. Regardless of your child's protests, if it walks like a duck, talks like a duck, and looks like a duck, it is a duck.

Even if you have not discovered drug paraphernalia, your son or daughter should be drug tested if you have noticed the smell of marijuana on or about your teen, in their car or their room; if they exhibit glassy, dazed eyes; if you observe a dramatic change in personality, including the need for excessive sleep, unusual hunger, or agitation and irritation – including anger outbursts, verbal insults and abuse, and a lack of motivation. Marijuana is not the only drug easily available to teenagers. Your local laboratory can test, through urine or blood, for many of the common drugs that teenagers get their hands on. But do not be fooled by a negative drug test. You should be aware that there are many ways to fool the test, especially if your teenager has been warned about monthly testing. Random drug tests are best, done on the same day they are announced. It is not all right for your adolescent to go to the laboratory with a "clean" friend, who will try to pass themselves off as your teenager when they provide the specimen.

It is worth mentioning here that if your teen has a penchant for getting high, he or she may try just about anything, including inhaling hair spray, lighter fluid and air-conditioning fluids. All of these are noxious to their system and, if done persistently and in escalating amounts, can cause serious injury and death.

Many teenagers will be punished for getting drunk and smoking pot, despite the fact that their parents behave in the same manner without retribution. You are the role model to your child, like it or not; if you can't control your negative impulses with regard to substance usage, you can be sure that your young adult will continue down the exact same path. Clean up your act or flush your teen's future down the drain.

Chapter 13

Boundaries

A ny conversation having to do with the word "bound-aries" almost always deteriorates into a miserable mess. Extremists believe that once a line is drawn in the sand it is permanent, without exception, forcing teenagers to tow the line or suffer the consequences. Advocates are more lenient, drawing boundary lines that can be pushed this way and pulled that way to fit almost any situation. Then there are opponents of all structure, who believe that teenagers should be encouraged to express themselves freely, regardless of the subject matter, and act in a manner in which the opinions and judgments of others are disregarded.

As if these views weren't confusing enough, we have the variables of each parent's personal views, brought into the marriage as baggage from their childhoods. Those who were raised strictly may believe that rigidity insures the ability to teach differentiation between right and wrong. Those who had a more relaxed childhood, with parents who flew by the seat of their pants, without plans or deadlines, without goals, boundary setting or parental follow-through, will have inadequately delineated teenage guidelines. Without parental structure, young adults are less inclined to develop necessary restraint and impulse control.

The truth is, children not only need but actually expect boundaries. That does not mean they uphold those boundaries, but they do expect some type of concrete order established by their parents as the foundation of their world.

Boundaries and Both Parents

Before you can expect your children to respect and obey the boundaries set in place, you and your spouse or other significant caregivers will have to come to a meeting of the minds. For those parents who are no longer married, what we are about to say still holds true. Regardless of geographic location and residential custody, parents – married or divorced – will be successful only with a consistently united front. We realize that in order to even attempt to do such a thing, those of you who are no longer married will have to actually decide to be mature and work together for the sake of the children. If you haven't already set aside your differences, why not agree to do so now, before your teenager becomes too old to parent? In our previous book, *In the Best Interest of the Child: A Manual for Divorcing Parents*, we detail the problems of single parenting with regard to raising emotionally healthy offspring during the turmoil and aftermath of divorce. If you are still having problems with your former spouse, you might want to pick up a copy of the book or visit us at our web site, www.inthebestin-terestofthechildren.com.

Assuming there are points of contention about one or more boundaries, both parents should list those line items that are most important to them, in order of priority; those which overlap should be less difficult to work on than those that appear on opposite ends of the priority spectrum. Universally problematic themes that arise with teens from every ethnic and socioeconomic level include curfew, bedtime, study habits, dating, smoking, driving, money, discipline and academic performance. Although you and your spouse or other significant caregiver will have individualized views, with a little bit of compromise and some philosophical adjustments, these views can unite. Until then, this chapter contains our thoughts, based on our experience, on these important subjects and their boundaries.

Bedtime and Curfew Boundaries

Don't expect bedtime designations and curfews to be well received, regardless of how much latitude you give. Studies show that children, teenagers and young adults require a minimum of eight hours of sleep, but most middle school and high school kids don't even come close to receiving the required amount of rest on week nights. Their school day begins several hours earlier than a teenager's biologic clock, and by the time they come home, grab a quick nap, complete their homework, maybe work at an after-school job, study for a test, and spend time on the computer and the phone, it is well past midnight by the time they shut their eyes.

Several recent studies by sleep researchers have concluded that because of their schedules and lifestyles many teenagers are deprived of approximately two hours each night of much-needed sleep. These sleep-deprived teens often attempt to make up that deficit by adding a nap to their after-school day, or by sleeping in on the weekends, often until one or two in the afternoon. Parents, concerned by their teen's "laziness," often blame their need for sleep on drugs or socialization overload, when, in fact, the teenager's biological clock does not crave sleep at night, but rather in the morning. During puberty there is a shift in the mechanisms controlling sleep which causes this desire to stay awake longer and sleep later. The sleep debt may actually worsen teenage aggression, lack of impulse control and poor decision making, as well as making their bodies more illness prone. Some teenagers have been mistakenly diagnosed with attention deficit disorder because of their inability to focus and concentrate due to sleep deprivation.

Many parents try to remedy this sleep deprivation by having a "lights out" rule by a certain hour. This may seem logical in your mind, but it doesn't compute in the mind of your teenager. Their argument is that they can't squeeze everything in that *has* to be done, and still eat dinner and watch a little television. Their argument holds water; they can't.

Teens are expected to not only excel academically but to participate in activities that help them become well-rounded. Therefore, they may need to stay after school for math tutoring or a basketball game; the first for academic assistance, the second for socialization or athletic skills, depending on whether they are watching or playing. They certainly must complete homework assignments and study for upcoming exams. We've already talked about the importance of their conversing with friends, and we are not big supporters of your teen working after school rather than having time for rest, homework, studying and socialization. That leaves dinner and television. We know they must eat, but what about television? If something has to go, shouldn't it be the boob tube?

Actually, we are going to have to lean toward the side of your teenagers. Television in moderation, and with guidance on the proper programming, is an excellent way to wind down, take a breather, and set aside the stress of the day. We do not support television viewed at the end of the evening in the comfort of their room while attempting to sleep. You cannot monitor the violence that is being hurled at your teenagers if the television is behind their closed doors, nor is it conducive to sleep to have adventure movies keeping them awake. Your children should be allowed some television exposure. Help them to plan out the evening and make program choices and times that fit into the rest of their schedule. In fact, we suggest that technological devices and electronic stimuli should not be located in your teens' bedrooms.

As for a "lights out" rule, we recommend allowing your teens to leave the lights on, as long as they are reading several chapters of a favorite book (not magazine). Reading a few chapters each night is one of the few things that should have been mandatory in your household from the time your children could read. If you haven't instituted a reading policy, do it now. Let the reader choose the book, as long as it is age appropriate, and encourage them to read. In fact, reward them for reading; this habit will be its own reward later in life.

Curfews almost always bring out the worst in teenage attitude; the argument is made that "things don't really get started until after 11:00 P.M. on a weekend." While that may be true, keep in mind that the average teen is wide awake during the hours when the average adult is in need of sleep. In order to keep your teenager off the roadways at times when there is an increase in drunken driving, and for you to know that they are home safely (by you actually *seeing* their physical presence and engaging them in conversation), you should make their curfew age-appropriate, noting geographical location and the norms of the community. That is not to say that because their friends can stay out until 1:00 A.M. you should cave in to that request. It is to say that in warmer, sunnier climates where daylight hours are longer and where it is not unusual for entire families to still be out and about well into the evening, your teen's curfew is likely to be somewhat later than that of a teen living in the tundra, where the sun goes down long before dinner and whole families hunker down for a long night. Also, curfews should be age appropriate; because your eighteen-year-old is allowed to stay out until midnight does not mean that your fifteen-year-old should have the same privilege. Only you can determine the maturity level of your offspring and whether their chronologic age matches their supposed level of responsibility. Err on the side of caution!

In your teenagers' defense, give them a fair curfew. If they are somewhat responsible, and they are going out to a movie, meeting with friends, or attending a concert, the rules can be adapted to the circumstances.

Generally, we advocate that teenagers should be at home on school nights, except for club meetings or sports events, and allowed an eleven or twelve o'clock curfew on Friday and Saturday nights, depending on your particular situation.

Study Boundaries

Study habits should be so ingrained by the time your child reaches puberty that it does not become a major point of contention. Some parents allow their children to study anywhere, as long as they put in their time; we do not agree. From our experience, a child should be seated at a desk or table, in a quiet room away from distraction, when they study. Studying in the middle of the kitchen when the rest of the family is talking, or studying in

Lazy? or Tired?

Ross came into therapy for "laziness" which his parents attributed to "poor genes." "He's just like his Uncle Roy, just like him. He ended up no damn good and Ross is walking right in his footsteps," his mother said. Their major complaint was Ross's inability to stay awake in class because of his insistence on staying up till midnight each night. Ross interrupted them, saying, "If you would just let me take a nap when I got home from school, I wouldn't fall asleep at the dinner table."

Both parents agreed that their son was sleep deprived, having to get up to catch the school bus by 5:30 A.M., but neither thought that Ross should take a nap "at his age." As soon as we assured the parents that Ross's sleep habits, although frustrating, were normal for his age, they agreed to allow him "naps without nagging" for one month. A month later, to the day, the family came into the office with a much more positive outlook on the character traits of their son. Once he had caught up on much-needed sleep, Ross became much more energized during his interactions with them, and in fact soon monopolized every conversation at the dinner table.

front of the television, is enough of a distraction that, although your child may swear they can only learn in the midst of chaos, be assured they are manipulating.

By the time they get into high school, your teenagers should be studying for at least one hour each night. They may say they have finished their homework, but if they don't bring a book home to review, or read ahead in preparation for the next chapter, they are slacking. A one-hour-minimum, mandatory study time will insure that your teen will study, because during that time they will not be allowed to do anything else. Make sure that the time set aside for studies corresponds to a time when a parent is going to be in attendance, for obvious reasons.

Often, parents say they will not oversee their teenager's work or remind them about a project because he or she should be old enough to take the responsibility for studying without assistance. Your child is never too old to need your help, and since you are their parent for the rest of your life, you do not get to arbitrarily decide an endpoint. Sorry. If you can see by their grades that they are having difficulty understanding a particular subject, and if you can help them, please do; if not, dig into your pocket and pay for tutoring. If your teenager balks at having a tutor, perhaps it is because they know they aren't trying their hardest; if they welcome your suggestion, you are on the right track and owe them whatever help a tutor can provide.

Dating

On the subject of dating, the majority of parents hope that their teen does not become involved in the dating ritual and the dramas that come along with dating until well into college. But, for most adolescents, puberty and attraction to the opposite sex go hand in hand. It is foolish to think that your teen son or daughter will be friends with everyone without having one exclusive partner, even though it may be as short-lived as a week or two. Even as recently as twenty years ago, dating was more innocent and naively romantic, without the pressing agenda of sex and possessiveness.

Like parents from generations before, you may not like your teen's partner choice, and you may try to break them apart. Perhaps a more constructive approach would be to get beyond the surface and see what the attraction is really about. If your child can control their partner, perhaps they have control issues that need evaluating. If your child is being controlled by their partner, perhaps their self-esteem is in question. Complementary partner choice is just that: the selection of a mate who possesses qualities that are considered desirable and necessary to complete the couple. You chose your partner this way, even if those attributes that you observed in your partner were generously awarded. Rather than trying to mask the problem by getting rid of your teenager's partner, which almost never works out the way you hope, why not assess the problem areas and have some short discussions with your son or daughter about these issues – not so much about your *concerns*, but about your *observations.* For example, if your daughter's boyfriend gets great joy out of pointing out her shortcomings and finds pleasure in laughing at her humiliation, you might say something along the lines of: "Do you think that Joe is trying to be mean when he calls attention to what he calls your clumsiness, or do you think he just doesn't know that it hurts your feelings?"

Then, even if your teenager rushes to Joe's defense, the point has been made and filed in her mental file cabinet. You do not have to belabor the point; she's got it.

Suppose your son's girlfriend constantly expects him to buy her gifts that he really can't afford. You might say something like: "Does it frustrate you that all the money you work hard for on your weekend job seems to be spent by Joan?" Again, even if your son rushes to defend his girlfriend or deny his overspending, he will rethink your observation and begin to wonder about her extravagant desires and how it might impact him (and his wallet) in the long run.

Conversely, there are parents who absolutely adore their teenager's partner choice, and who erroneously believe that their child will remain happily linked to this person forever. This thinking is not only foolish, but it sends a wrong message. Teenage love is sweet, innocent, passionate and all-consuming when it is good, and over when it is over. None of us should encourage young people to lock into any partner choice at this age without experiencing all types of relationships – weighing each relationship's strengths and weaknesses until they find the proper choice for them. With a little bit of luck, this will not happen until your teenager has matriculated through college and beyond.

You should not stay in contact with your teenager's former love interest unless he or she does. Otherwise, let this previous relationship move on, and allow your teen to choose their own friends. Your adolescent's ex-partner may be a great girl or guy, but they are not *your* friend.

Sex and the Teenager

A few thoughts on the sexual revolution:

- Just when you think it can't get any more brazen or bold, think again.
- Teenage sex has reached all-time highs, with teens as young as twelve and thirteen participating in sexual acts that some of us didn't even hear about until well into adulthood.
- Whether it is societal permissiveness, accessibility to unsupervised homes, availability of sexually explicit material, or peer pressure, if your son or daughter is looking for sex, it will not be too difficult to find.

Explanations about the importance of waiting until marriage to have sex didn't work when we were growing up, and they aren't working now. This is not to say there isn't a minority of teens who has chosen chastity until marriage, but the majority *has* experimented with sex, at least infrequently. The main worry just three decades ago was the possibility of contracting a sexually transmitted disease, such as syphilis or gonorrhea, or the real threat of teenage pregnancy and bringing an illegitimate child into the world. With the advent of birth control pills in the 1960s, and more recently with the legalization of abortion clinics, medicines to cure STDs, and the privacy act of HIPPA (Healthcare Information Portability and Accountability Act), teens in many states can get birth control, abortions and medication for themselves, without their parents' knowledge or consent.

In the twenty-first century, AIDS is the real and tragic challenge facing our youngsters who are having unprotected sex. With the availability of condoms, there is absolutely no reason to have sex without using protection, yet despite school sex education classes, parent-child discussions, and mass media announcements, teenagers seem more intent on satisfying immediate sexual urges than on protecting their lives.

Those of you who believe that your child is not having sex may be correct, but then again you may be wrong. The fact that your teen doesn't confide his or her sexual history to you is not proof that they are not sexually active. If they have been in a long-term relationship, the statistics that support abstinence are even more dismal. Even a "good teenager," raised "properly," from a "good family" may have a sexual encounter during what used to be called a "one-night stand." In fact, there is a term commonly circulating among the teen set called "friends with benefits." This term is self-explanatory. The obvious problems to "friends with benefits" are all of the points we have already mentioned, as well as one important concept that has not been adequately addressed, namely, the emotional injury that comes from having indiscriminate and careless sex.

There are no standard responses or magical remedies to "cure" the sexual dilemmas that your teenagers face except for you to be available to them when they want to talk, listening to them without expressing shock if you want truthful answers.

Questions about birth control and the like will not be discussed in this book, but there are family doctors, specialists and clinics that will be more than happy to speak with you privately with regard to your concerns. The most important point is this: Your teenagers do not know as much as they think they do, nor are they equipped emotionally to handle their sexual urges and the consequences. As we mentioned in a previous chapter, the best answer is supervision and the lack of opportunity.

Even with a parent in residence, your children should never be allowed to entertain anyone in their bedroom with the bedroom door closed, which goes for the bathroom as well. Consider any closed or locked door a red flag. For those of you who don't think this is the case, try walking in unannounced. You may get the shock of your life. No doubt your teenagers will request some privacy, a place where they and their friend can "talk" without parental or sibling interference. Suggest the back yard, the front yard, the family room (if you have one), or even two lawn chairs pulled up in the driveway, but do not fall for the "need for privacy in my room" routine. That "conversation" may wind up taking nine months, with the result defining your teenager's future for years to come.

Boundaries Around Money

This would be a good time to discuss money, since dating and not having enough money go hand in hand. If your teenager does not work, then they probably don't have a regular source of income. Your son or daughter may be too old to get an allowance, but they need pocket money. Find a budget that seems reasonable, and give them enough money to not embarrass them. Nothing is worse than your son not having enough money to purchase two movie tickets when he wants to take his girlfriend out on a Friday night, or your daughter finding herself without money to join her friends for a night of pizza and bowling. Dating in the twenty-first century cannot be measured against dating norms from a few decades ago, when a male was expected to be financially responsible for paying for his date. Today's teenagers generally have a mutual understanding that although there are times when a girl can expect a boyfriend to pay for a movie or dinner, for the most part, the expenses are shared. This has come to pass neither from selfishness nor poor etiquette, but rather from an escalating economy that has prices skyrocketing. Your teenager

About Ted

Teens and their parents often fight about money, or the lack of it. In many cases parents expect their offspring to either earn money for clothing or entertainment, or do without. This philosophy has damaged many parent/teen bonds, not to mention thwarted normal socialization.

Take Ted, for instance. Ted's parents, although upper-middle class, were both raised in families in which money was tight, and although that is not the case now, they both hold onto every dime they make, depriving not only their children but themselves some of the pleasures that money can buy. They have never taken a family vacation, will not spend money to have their family portrait taken, refuse to eat in restaurants, and bring brown-bag lunches to work every day. Mrs. M. has worn the same five dresses, now faded, to work every day for the past two years, while Mr. M. shops for any clothing he might need in thrift stores. They have more than half a million dollars in their retirement fund, and yet they feel anxious about their financial future. Ted worked is going to need money in pocket, without question. Where this money comes from is the question.

If your son or daughter has worked throughout the summer and during vacations or has a part time job – dog-sitting or car-washing – this money can be added to the money you are going to give them. If you really don't have any extra money, or are so strapped that you cannot pay your bills, no one expects you to go bankrupt funding your kid, but many parents we have seen in our practice throughout the years say one thing and do another. If you are not helping your child financially but you're shopping for clothing, getting your hair and nails done, taking vacations, and driving a new car, we are not going to believe that you can't help your teen, and neither are they.

for two years every day after school to have enough money to purchase a ten-year-old "junker" car that breaks down regularly. It then sits in the yard until Ted makes enough money to pay for a part and for a mechanic to get it running until the next time it breaks down. What money he might have spent on clothing in order to feel better about himself, as compared to his peers, is sucked into the money pit of his car. But without his car he would not be able to get to work.

Ted didn't see a way out of this trap, and he accepted his lot in life until he met Margie, the new girl in school, who seemed to like him. He begged his parents for money to take her out on a date, but they refused. He asked for more hours at work but it was the slow season, and the company was cutting back. Embarrassed by the position in which he found himself, Ted avoided Margie's flirtations until she became convinced that Ted was simply not interested, and found herself another boyfriend – one who had more confidence and more options for dating.

There is no doubt that children are a bottomless pit in which money is thrown only to disappear, but no one said raising a child was either easy or cheap. Teenagers need money; that is a fact of life. However, they don't need too much money. The parent who gives an adolescent excessive amounts of money not only skews their teen's ability to appreciate the value of a dollar, but also invites trouble. For example, it is difficult to purchase drugs without a pocketful of change; be aware of exactly where the money you give your child is going.

There is a fine line between too much and too little when it comes to money, and neither is good. Do not discourage your teenager from dreaming about the finer things in life, because those goals may be attainable with hard work and perseverance someday. Neither should you encourage your child to seek out friends, employment or a partner simply because there is a hefty sum of money which accompanies these choices. Remember, money does not buy happiness, but it does buy trouble.

Driving a Car

Depending on where you live, your teenager will be granted either a permit or a driver's license at a young age. Interestingly, some children are less than thrilled about driving. We say that because there are always a few teenagers who put off getting their license for various reasons. This doesn't always follow the plan of parents who mark the calendar for the day when their offspring can drive, excited to be able to delegate some of the carpooling and shopping. If your son or daughter does not want to get their license, they must have their reasons. Perhaps they know they are not mature enough to drive; perhaps they fear having an accident, or don't want to be responsible for carting around their friends. That's fine. Any teenager who is reluctant to stand in line at the Motor Vehicle Department on the day they are legally able to drive is actually displaying good judgment.

You may be burdened with the driving chores for another year or more, but your teen will not be the cause of an accident, at least for the time being.

When your teenager drives, you can expect them to have at least one fender-bender. No one wants this to occur, but it probably will, and it will more than likely be their fault. If they are preoccupied with the cell phone or the radio; if they are blasting music so loudly that they can't think straight; if they are laughing and fooling around with their passengers, they are an accident waiting to happen. Your teen's cell phone should be used only in an emergency if they are behind the wheel of a vehicle. In fact, using a cell phone while driving is illegal in many areas. If you find out that your teen disregards this rule, you have good reason to separate them from their car for at least one day as a gentle reminder of your wishes.

If your teenager gets a parking ticket, speeding ticket, or is involved in a fender-bender, try to keep your reaction in perspective and help them use it as a learning experience. If he or she gets ticketed for careless driving, it is time to tighten the reins a little, and perhaps enroll them in a private driving course. If they have a paying job, have them contribute a portion of their paycheck toward the course fee. They will be humiliated enough to be driving around with "Student Driver" clearly stamped all over the body of the vehicle. Taking a few dollars from their paycheck will better reinforce the experience.

As we've noted throughout this book, the key to discipline is consistency and swift action. If your teenager has committed an infraction that deserves a punishment (refer to your behavior-consequence chart), be swift in the administration of that punishment. Although we do believe there will have to be some parental wisdom involved in a conversational exchange with your son or daughter, do not belabor the point. You are not dealing with someone who is unable to understand the spoken word; make your point clearly and be finished. He or she will not have time to tune out your voice or your message if it is short and sweet.

Owning a Cell Phone

Should your teenager have a cell phone? Yes. Should you monitor the calls and have a cut-off time each night? Yes.

Because your teens carry their own cell phones does not make them rightfully theirs. The cell phone is your property and it is their privilege to speak with their friends.

Many schools do not allow cell phones on the campus; others allow phones only if they are placed on vibrate or are turned off during class time. Find out what your school's policy is on cell phones, and honor it. If you help your teenagers hide their cell phones, you teach them nothing except that you are a co-conspirator in breaching rules and regulations.

If there is good reason for your son or daughter to have a cell phone in school – for example, a relative who is very sick or dying, or a medical problem that may require immediate contact with a parent (such as juvenile diabetes that often gives rise to unsteady blood sugar levels) – go to the school and work something out with the administration. They will be glad to assist with any emergency exceptions as long as they are informed.

Get Organized

With so many variables crowding the day, and so many goals to achieve, boundaries are definitely important. Nothing can be accomplished with disorganization and distraction except further turmoil and chaos. If your household seems exceptionally chaotic, take the time to re-evaluate the boundaries that are in place, as well as your discipline practices, and restructure whenever necessary. If you can't do this without assistance, ask for help from your spouse or from your school resource assistants – such as guidance counselors – to formulate a plan for positive years ahead.

Chapter 14
Your Adolescent's Health

Once your child begins developing secondary sex characteristics, such as facial hair in boys and breasts in girls, they should be taken to their physician for their yearly physical checkup. Just because they haven't been ill recently doesn't mean they shouldn't have a thorough physical examination, including blood work, every year. We mention this because in many families, as children outgrow their childhood illnesses, taking them to the doctor is no longer a part of the routine. Yet, during puberty and young adulthood, disorders can manifest. If your adolescent has not had a routine blood test within the last year, be sure that you ask your physician to test them. Before you send your son or daughter off to college, you want to make sure there are no medical problems lurking about. College is stressful enough without being plagued with illness.

One of the illnesses that is more common during the teenage years is mononucleosis, often called the "kissing disease," although the spread of "mono" and kissing are not always paired. Also, especially in female children, a blood test will confirm any iron deficiency anemia, which is more common in menstruating females, especially if they have a heavy flow. Staph infections known as MRSA that infect the skin and are easily passed on have been in the news of late. The spread of this infection was previously thought to be due to a staph-resistant organism only found in hospitals. Now, this same infection is becoming more common in schools, especially among those involved in contact sports such as wrestling. If your child develops a sore that looks nasty and does not heal quickly, there is no time to be lost. Take

123

him or her to a physician for wound cultures and proper antibiotic treatment.

Conditions such as anemia, more common in females because of heavy menstrual flow, could be the reason your teenager is having difficulty with energy and concentration. Also, thyroid disorders and other endocrine abnormalities can play a part in the disruption of normal activity, sleep, concentration and focus.

If you are the parent of a female, add a gynecologist to the roster of your child's doctors as soon as puberty is reached. Your daughter needs a regular gynecological checkup. Your doctor may or may not choose to perform an invasive examination and pap smear, but at the least, an annual trip to the gynecologist should become a routine event so that your daughter is easily introduced to the necessity of breast exams and pap smears.

Birth control information can be readily obtained at the gynecologist's office as well. We are neither supporting nor undermining the need for birth control, simply mentioning that it is available from physicians, as well as from free clinics and through the health department in your particular area.

When you take your teenager to the pediatrician or internal medicine doctor (if your pediatrician has an age cut-off), share any concerns you have with him or her. Although most doctors uphold the right to your child's privacy and patient/doctor confidentiality, your teen can sign a request allowing open conversation among all of you. In some states, until your child reaches the age of maturity the pediatrician is not bound by confidentiality, but it is always best in the teen years to have an open policy by which your child's doctors can share test results and findings.

Your Teen's Physical Appearance

Teenagers are narcissistic, so you can anticipate that yours are probably never going to be pleased with their appearance. However, in some cases, your teens may have a good point. Whether the social system and job market are fair or skewed, for the most part statistics show that people who are thin and handsome have more friends and better job opportunities than those who aren't. It's difficult enough to be in the running for good jobs without being tossed aside because of a physical obstacle.

If your son is unfortunate enough to have inherited his uncle's floppy ears, or your daughter has inherited her aunt's huge nose, their self-esteem may have taken quite a beating from peers. No one is suggesting that you encourage vanity, but through the marvels of modern medicine, your child does not have to live under the confines of a hat in order to be social. If your teenager has asked to have his or her features reconstructed, and you believe that their life would be immeasurably happier without being called names, please take them to a reputable plastic surgeon ... make that two reputable plastic surgeons ... for their opinions, keeping in mind that all surgeries, regardless of how routine they are, always carry a risk of infection, complications, and, at times, death. If you believe your offspring would fare better in the world without the strawberry patch birthmark that covers an otherwise beautiful face, make the appointment. Remember, you get what you pay for in life, and a good plastic surgeon is not going to come cheap. But if this means lifelong happiness for your child, make the investment in their future.

While we're on the subject, in our opinion, breast implants do not qualify as a reason to put your child at risk on a surgical table. It may be true that well-endowed women get more attention, and possibly even more job options, but your daughter may get a whole lot more than you imagined, having nothing to do with employment opportunity.

Before you select any physician for your child, be it pediatrician, internal medicine specialist, gynecologist or plastic surgeon, make sure they are Board Certified in their field of expertise. Check out their credentials as well as their track record by calling your local hospital as well as the licensing board in your state; any lawsuits or infractions are a matter of public record and you may be surprised at what you find. Most people do more research when purchasing a car than when selecting a physician, which makes no sense at all.

Eating Disorders

One of the overt signs of the eating disorder known as *anorexia nervosa* is a physique that is much too thin for the frame of your teenager's body. We mention this because other signs, such as a decrease in food ingestion, may be completely hidden, especially in such busy times in which families often cannot sit down and eat meals together. Anorexia is a symptom of a much deeper and underlying disorder; it is also a very serious illness that can lead to death. If you notice your teenager refusing to eat, or picking at food or if his or her body seems to be "wasting away," you should make an appointment with a professional for evaluation. Admittedly, when most people think of anorexia and its cousin bulimia (binge eating followed by vomiting), they think of them as strictly female disorders, but that is not always the case.

Your teen needs sustenance. Foregoing occasional meals is one thing, but refusal to eat, or running to the bathroom to vomit after every meal is a sign of a dire emergency. Often parents will become angry at their teen, as if he or she is punishing them directly by not eating. It may be true that your offspring harbors resentment toward one or both you, but generally the anger and depression go much deeper than that. An evaluation by a clinical psychologist may include the recommendation that your teen spend some time in a facility that treats eating disorders. Should that be the case, please adhere to the request of the doctor or other professional for the sake of your child's well-being.

Steroid Use

In male children there is generally a growth spurt that occurs somewhere around fifteen to eighteen years of age, followed by a "filling out" period. This does not translate into "bulking up." "Filling out" means that those who were once scrawny have now become more "meaty."

If your son works out at a local gym and is faithful about exercising regularly and maintaining a healthy diet, these are good things that will lead to results that would be considered "normal" filling out. Excessive "bulking up" is, well, excessive, and may be an indication of steroid use.

Common symptoms of steroid use may also include irritability, aggressiveness, agitation, and a thick neck and excessively muscular arms, upper body and legs. If you are concerned, your physician should be consulted. Tests can be run to determine steroid use; and regardless of what your son tells you, steroids are not his friend.

Testing for Drug Use

Observation is the key to insight when it comes to teenagers, and we are convinced it is also the reason we humans were given all five senses. Use them. Look into your teen's eyes. Are they bloodshot or glassed over? Are they reddened? If so, you should suspect some type of drug or alcohol usage. Try to set your preconceived judgments aside – the ones that spew forth and sound like, "No child of mine would ever do drugs." *Any* child of *anyone* might experiment with drugs, and depending on the drug of choice, they may not be able to stop.

Marijuana use is common among teenagers, and is probably most often the drug of choice, but we cannot disregard uppers, downers, LSD, prescription drugs and pain killers. Street drugs such as cocaine and heroin are quickly addictive, as is the prescription drug Oxycodone. These drugs are capable of completely ruining your child's future. For this reason, if your son or daughter is using drugs, they should be regularly and randomly drug tested by your physician.

Emotional Health

Now that we have your teenager's physical appearance and health addressed, we should examine their habits. If your child seems edgy, irritable, hyperactive, overly sensitive, aggressive, overly moody, depressed, withdrawn, isolated, emotionally volatile, or anxious, it is your job as the parent to look into the situation; and by this we do not mean hope it is a phase that will pass. We mean solicit outside help from every resource available, including teachers, physicians, mental health counselors and psychologists. While the teen years are known to be volatile and unstable, this instability is within moderation; anything excessive is suspect. You do not have the credentials to determine what is moderation and what is suspect, but one of the above resources can guide you. (Refer to Chapter 5, Teen Anxiety, for more on this vital subject, and see the section on resources at the end of this book.)

Have Courage

As we have stated throughout this book, parenting is not for the faint of heart; you must be vigilant about sticking to your standards and values even in the face of adversity. Because everyone else is allowing their children to participate in some things doesn't make it right. On the other hand, if you are not reasonable in your demands, you will have a lot more problems on your hands than you do already.

Chapter 15

Academic Needs

Academic performance is another sticky wicket. On one hand, you believe your teen is as able-bodied, intelligent, witty and capable as the next person because you are their parent. But, just as quickly, you wonder how on earth they have made it through school thus far.

Undoubtedly, most teenagers do not have the internal focus and drive that motivates them to excel; they tend to have good intentions, but slack off within a few weeks of work, losing sight of the goal. Many of them view school itself as a punishment, and will quickly offer valid explanations that courses such as algebra or history are never going to be used in their lifetime. *Ah, youth, how quickly they grow up eating their words.* Still, although they may be correct on some level, your teenagers will not be called upon to revamp the school system anytime soon, and therefore will have to play by the school's rules.

In our clinical practice counseling teens we have spent many collective hours with teenagers who believe they know everything they need to know to get along just fine in the world, only to meet up with them and their anxiety five or ten years later when they recognize that they know nothing! Wisdom and experience go hand in hand, but neither can be passed down easily. Most adolescents vehemently struggle to fight their own battles, forge their own paths, and make their own mistakes – mistakes that would have been preventable if only they had listened. Fortunately for everyone concerned, this rebellious and autonomous phase passes relatively quickly and is sometimes followed by a phase in which the adult children come running back to the safety of the nest.

For the most part, encourage your teenagers to do the best they can academically. Ask them to strive for B's if they are good students and to accept C's if they are average students. An A-grade is a sign of perfection, and just because your child was able to ace their courses through second and third grade, don't expect the same to be true in middle and high school. High school courses are really complicated and difficult for many teens. In many schools there is a concept called "tracking"; a "track" is another word for "level." If your teenagers are in honors classes they are considered in many high schools to be on the "high" or "top" track. Conversely, if your child is barely passing and has problems with retention of material, test taking and comprehension, they may be on the "low" or "bottom" track. If your son or daughter attends a school where they are able to "track" more advanced learning, and they can actually learn the material without too much sacrifice in other equally important areas, that is fine, but remember that an A in an average track will probably not equate to the same grade in an advanced track.

Parents often treat poor grades punitively, but do not use good grades as an incentive for rewards. If your child has received a bad grade on a test or report card, certainly something is going to have to change, but rather than thinking of a punishment, such as taking away their car or money, why not structure a better system of studying, or fewer hours devoted to sports and more to academics? If you don't act like you are giving out a consequence as you revamp your teenager's activities, but present the new activity with a positive slant, you can work together as a family to find out where the kinks are in the academic department and repair them. Your teenagers do not want to bring home poor grades; they worry about it, suffer for it, and are embarrassed in front of their peers. If they are not doing well, they will "punish" themselves. It is your job to guide them in constructive ways.

Help Them

If your teenager is having difficulty with academic organizational skills, test taking, studying, or understanding and/or retaining specific course information, the first step is to make an appointment with his or her teachers. Before going to this meeting, compile a list of your concerns or observations, because your time may be somewhat limited. Don't forget that, as much as your child's teachers want to help your teen, realistically they have hundreds of students who need equal time and concern. Question the teachers about their observations: Does he think your teenager is preoccupied, distracted, uninterested, bored, or struggling? Does she offer her time either before or after school for those students who need extra help? Does he have suggestions for better study habits or classroom decorum? If a teacher believes your child is impertinent or disrespectful, ask for specific examples and write them down so you can discuss these behaviors with your teenager at home.

Human nature being what it is, not every one person will get along with every other person on the planet, or in this case, in the classroom. However, because of the hierarchy, the student is to be respectful of the teacher; that means, even if your son or daughter does not like a teacher, or thinks he or she is mean or gives too much homework, unless this teacher specifically targets your child unfairly and consistently, your adolescent will simply have to recognize that they will either have to acquiesce to the teacher's wishes or suffer the consequences. For the most part, it would require too much effort (by the teacher) for very little gain to target one child with the goal of making this student's life miserable for the entire school year. That said, however, as in every walk of life, there may be a teacher who is burned out or who has a negative transference of emotions onto your child. If after weighing all the evidence you believe that is the case, you have a duty to bring your findings to the principle or head of the school.

Assuming that you trust the observations of your child's teachers and follow their directions, if the problem persists, there are several recourses. If your teenager is having difficulty in one specific subject, find out if the school offers a tutoring program; if not, there are often retired educators or even students who can be hired to help out. If your adolescent's academic problems are more global, and he or she appears unable to grasp the concept of prioritizing studies or has difficulties completing assignments and passing tests, there may be facilities (such as The Sylvan Learning Center, to name one) in your area or a surrounding area that can be quite helpful. These services or programs may come with a high price tag, but the success of your child will be worth the investment.

If your child still cannot concentrate for studies and test taking, it might be time to take them to a licensed clinical psychologist who can administer tests to diagnose any hidden problems, such as depression, anxiety, attention deficit disorder or a learning disability. If you do not know how to locate a tutor, and your telephone book doesn't specifically have a heading that can assist you, ask your teenager's guidance counselor for the names and telephone numbers of both tutors and tutoring institutions in your neighborhood.

College Prep

By the time your young teenager has begun high school, we hope that the notion of attending college is an expected extension of his or her educational process and not some obscure pipe dream. In today's world, higher education is the key to opening the doors of opportunity. What a bachelor's degree is today is equivalent to what a high school diploma was four decades ago; without it, not only will your son or daughter have less opportunity against competition in the workplace, their salary will be commensurate with their level of education. It is difficult enough for someone to make ends meet if they're making optimal money, but without an education, your teen may be forced to work two or even three jobs just to pay the bills.

The reverse side of the argument is this: Not all young people are cut out for college. Due to immaturity, lack of commitment, intellectual difficulties, or a desire to delay their academic pursuits to gain "hands on" knowledge, to travel or pursue specific dreams – such as acting talents or missionary work – your encouragement will go a long way in both supporting their ambitions and allowing the maturation process to give them a more indepth appreciation for higher education once they return to the academic arena – or not. Not all teenagers matriculate on to higher education. Fortunately, having a talent for and interest in a skilled trade can still open doors of opportunity. Being a master carpenter or plumber is not lower on the list of employment, but it is more physically demanding and increases the probability of job-related injury. However, whether your child's talents lie in law, medicine, retail, or the restaurant business, the most important piece of advice you can give them is that no amount of education is ever wasted; to broaden their horizons, accruing knowledge should not terminate upon high school graduation.

Money is not a reason to turn away from college. There are many colleges that offer private grants and "free money" not only to academic geniuses but to those students who have a sincere desire to learn. Go to your local bookseller and read through books on college grants and loans; you may be surprised to see large national corporations giving, not lending, money for reasons that include, but are not limited to, academic success. Even if your teenager has to take out a student loan, it will be well worth it in the long run, so long as their choice of major culminates in a paid position and not expertise in an obscure interest.

Guidance counselors today are stretched past their limits, as are teachers. They are busy correcting schedules and moving students in and out of class, as well as taking on behavior problems. Perhaps in some schools that are less crowded, guidance counselors can still give individualized attention to each and every student, but it has been our experience that many students of junior high and high school age students are uninformed as to their options and futures unless their parents push them into a direction, or specifically ask for guidance. It is true that academic and scholarship information is available in the guidance office if a teenager is motivated to look for it, but most teenagers do not have a grasp of the broad spectrum of what is available. They don't know what they don't know, and therefore don't know that there is anything to seek. Sadly, it is the exception more than the rule that teens and their parents are equipped with adequate knowledge with regard to their academic future and its opportunities.

Admissions Info

A word on the admissions packets to college: You can send for them in the mail or download them from the Internet, but either way your teenager is going to require your help in filling out the paperwork. It is boring and tedious, and he or she is often not mature enough to settle down to the kind of commitment it takes to fill out the forms properly and get them where they need to go in a timely manner. Also, these admission applications need to have a check or credit card number attached. Submitting admissions is an expensive proposition, but if your child limits themselves to only one or two colleges, they may be out of the running when acceptance time comes rolling around. They should apply to one or two of their "absolute favorite" schools, plus one college that is probably not within their reach, and several that they are likely to be accepted to, even if these are not their first or second choice.

Remember, the farther away the college, the more cost to you for travel, care packages, and other needs that might otherwise

Keira and College

Keira was depressed because most of her friends were planning to leave town within a few months of graduation from high school. These were peers she had known throughout her entire school career, and all were matriculating to universities. Keira's parents were poor, and neither had graduated high school. To them, the fact that Keira was getting her diploma was enough of an accomplishment. Keira planned to help out in a local attorney's office as a file clerk, with the possibility of someday moving up to receptionist. Although she would see her friends on their winter and spring breaks, she knew it would never be the same – since their lives were heading toward endless possibilities, while it felt to her that her life was never going to be any different.

Keira was not only intelligent and hard working but mature and well spoken, but that alone was not enough to get her where she needed to be. We told her that college was not out of the question, that there were scholarships and grants, and that major companies had "free money" for students who applied. Eagerly, she buried her head in scholarship books borrowed from the local library and applied to colleges. She babysat for the application fees and wrote heartfelt letters which accompanied her applications, stating her academic dreams and her willingness to work hard. She then asked for a miracle.

She got one! Actually she got three. Three universities accepted Keira. She chose one close to home so that transportation costs would not be an added burden. She was also delighted to learn that many of her peers would be joining her on this nearby campus in the fall.

be avoided if they attended a college closer to home. That is not to discourage your teenager from reaching for the stars, just to let them know that balancing a budget is a part of residing on planet Earth. If they do choose to go to a college that is at least one plane ride away, be straight with them (prior to accepting) about how often they can expect to come home. School is generally closed for Thanksgiving and Christmas holidays, and often for full summer breaks. During the summer, dormitory rooms often have to be emptied, which means that, unless your offspring lives in an apartment, his or her belongings will have to be moved, stored, and returned to campus when school starts again in the fall.

Chapter 16
Serious Trouble

The teenage behaviors we have addressed so far, although irritating and worrisome, still fall within the range of normal. However, there are times when you will have to evaluate whether your child has crossed the line from what is considered "normal" to what is not. To a certain degree, teenagers would not be teenagers without some opposition and defiance, but if the degree to which they rebel is out of control and extreme, they are likely experiencing other difficulties that may not yet been identified. A professional psychologist will evaluate and treat your teenager, as well as assist you in coping with their "over the top" anger, rage, and defiance until they find resolution. Do not think a teenager will simply outgrow these areas of concern. To the contrary, this negative behavior will often increase in frequency and escalate in intensity as he or she matures.

A Climate of Fear

In previous chapters we have offered you guidance about structure, boundary setting and consequence application, but some of you may fear your teenagers and therefore be reluctant to enforce what you have learned. In the event that no one has told you this before, *you should never be afraid of your teenager.*

No one should have to live with fear, threats and abuse. You may feel trapped in your belief that there is no solution, that because you are the parent you will have to tolerate this type of behavior from your teenager. *You do not.* Consult an attorney and seek a court injunction if necessary, and allow the system to place your son or daughter in therapy, boot camp, survival camp, boarding school or a state-run facility for delinquents, offenders and behavior problems. You are not doing either of you a favor by tolerating your teen's dysfunctional behavior in the hope that they will outgrow their abusiveness; further, you will be sending this angry person out into society where they will inflict their rage on others. If he is terrorizing you today, he will terrorize a wife, child or co-worker tomorrow.

Although many assume that perpetrators of violence and aggression are male, there has been a shift in that thinking in the past decade. Men often have to deal with girlfriends or spouses who are emotionally and physically abusive. Regardless of the root of their aggression, more females are acting out against their male partners, as well as other females, with behaviors that range from hair pulling and physical assault to actual murder. Parents today often feel quite threatened by their female children, yet they underestimate their intentions and aggression. The bottom line is this: No adolescent, regardless of gender or age, should ever make or imply any threats or aggressive actions toward any member of their household, school or community without immediate intervention and professional evaluation and treatment.

Serious Business
Theft
A young person who commits an act such as stealing is committing a crime. Such acts are not "pranks," and should not be minimized by labeling them as such. There is a legal and moral distinction between generalized adolescent mischief and a criminal act. One is punished within the confines of the home and the other is punished in a court of law.

Fires
Along with theft, firesetting is another abnormal activity that usually starts in childhood, and, if not treated, can become pyromania – the need and desire to set fires. If your child has a preoccupation

with fires but channels it into a constructive career, he or she may become a valued member of a fire department someday, but if they cannot control the impulse to set a fire, they are committing a criminal act that has tremendous and far-reaching emotional and financial consequences, including the loss of life.

Violence to Animals

Hurting animals is becoming increasingly more common, and is escalating into purposefully heinous, unthinkable acts against helpless creatures that have put their trust in humankind. A teenager who hunts down domestic animals for sport, ties them up, skins them, drags them behind cars, or worse is likely to later abuse humans in similar fashion. Animals cannot speak for themselves and often are at the mercy of humans. If your child abuses animals, they are harboring repressed anger and rage that must be treated immediately. Animal cruelty is against the law.

Abuse – Sexual or Otherwise

Child abuse or child molestation is not only abnormal, but must be reported. If you know that your child has molested or abused another teenager or younger child and you do not turn him or her into the authorities, you are setting them up for escalating dysfunction and putting one more dangerous person onto already crowded, dysfunctional streets. With crimes such as these, you are going to have to step outside your parental nurturing role and report your teenager for the better good of society. If you do not, you can be certain that with the next child they abuse – and there will surely be another innocent victim – the abuse will be as much your fault as the perpetrator's.

Truancy

At one time or another, teenagers push the discipline envelope and decide they can skirt the rules by skipping school, which is a punishable offense. If the occurrence is a one-time event, you do not have that much to be concerned about. Truancy, however, is another event entirely. Truancy is the continual absence of your teens from their classes, and must be dealt with not only by the school, but by you.

Do not lie for your kids and send them to school with notes of deceit, outlining everything from fictitious sore throats to a death in the family. If your teenagers have taken it upon themselves to not show up for class, they will have to take the punishment for their actions. Covering for them teaches them nothing except that they now have an accomplice to their crime.

Pornography

Pornography is a serious topic. On one hand, teenagers are driven by natural curiosity and raging hormones, lured to what is forbidden. In days gone by a young boy might have taken a peak at a "dirty" magazine but later outgrew this phase as he matured toward the need for intimacy with a partner. However, things have changed in the twenty-first century. With access to Internet pornography comes an increasingly alarming number of viewers with an insatiable need for eroticism, which often escalates into full-blown addiction. Internet pornography and chat rooms are climbing the charts as the reason for severed relationships and marriages. Internet sex also transforms sexual activity from something that was once intimate – between two consenting adults – into physical aggression, immoral acts and escalating addiction, leaving any form of intimacy behind.

Depression, Anxiety, Suicide

Last, and most important, as we discussed at length in Chapter 5, "Teen Anxiety," teenagers can and do suffer from depression and anxiety. There may be a specific concern to which the depression is connected, such as parental divorce, which rocks even the most solid foundation of an adolescent's life, or the depression may be all-consuming but generalized. It is not too soon to take your adolescent to a reputable, licensed clinical psychologist to be evaluated and treated if you have any reason to suspect depression and anxiety beyond the predictable ups and downs. If therapy alone doesn't work, then the therapist may suggest that your child receive therapy in conjunction with psychotropic medication.

Kids can and do try to commit suicide, and they often succeed. Many parents consider the threat of suicide to be a manipulative ploy for attention, and they may be right, but even a "staged" suicide can go horribly wrong, with death the end result. If your child appears extremely depressed, or makes any threats or comments, to you or anyone else, about thinking about, planning or executing a suicide, take them to the nearest emergency room or call the police immediately; tomorrow may be too late. This one irreversible act may be prevented provided that you have watched for clues of deteriorating behavior and taken your teenager's threats seriously.

With or without your consent, the police may commit your teen to the hospital for psychiatric evaluation if the young person is believed to be a danger to themselves or others. A hospital admission will put your child safely under professional supervision for a minimum of seventy-two hours, during which time he or she can be evaluated and treated. If the psychiatrist believes that your teenager needs continued intensive care, a court order will place him or her in a facility until such time as they are determined to be of sound mind and body.

Formally or not, by virtue of giving birth to or adopting your child you have taken a parental "oath" to keep them safe from harm if at all in your power. Your acting swiftly, even if that act is erring on the side of caution, can give your son or daughter a second chance at their future. If your teen was manipulating you by throwing the "suicide card" on the table, they will get the education of their life after spending three days in a psychiatric facility – an education they won't soon forget.

Chapter 17

A Family Epic

Those of you who are about to embark on the journey of parenting a teenager may look on with envy at those families who are closing in on the final chapters of their children's adolescence. Yet, surprising even to themselves, these "finishing" parents are actually envious of you. They appreciate that although you have already made some mistakes, you still have time to set things right in your own house and construct boundaries that are reasonable and fair, yet rugged enough not to fold under the strain of emotional volatility.

Based on our practice, we know quite a few families who have been successful in learning how to set limits and maintain boundary consistency, reinstating familial harmony as a result. Why don't we take a peek at how a hypothetical family (a composite of several of our real-life cases) worked out their conflicts with their teenage son and daughter? The mother's (Eileen's) reflections *are written in italics;* and those of the father, John, are in regular font.

I wanted to get married and have children since the time I was old enough to play house. I think I can speak for John when I say he felt the same way. We met later in life, after we had both been divorced, and because neither of us was blessed with children, we thought we shouldn't waste any time starting a family. Within the first two years of marriage, both of our children were born. The first, a boy, we named Cody. Our little girl we named Jenny. We didn't have too much to worry about financially, so we hired a nanny to help out. Both of us had careers which needed quite a bit of our attention. It all seemed to work out all right in the beginning.

When Eileen and I met, I was just coming out of a nasty divorce; she had been single for about three years and had put her divorce behind her. For me, Eileen was a really quick decision. I'm not saying I married her on the rebound, but I sometimes wonder if I should have stayed single a little longer. I just didn't like coming home to an empty house with no one to talk to or eat dinner with. From the first night we met she wanted us to be a couple, but we weren't married a week before she wanted to try having kids. I didn't say no . . . I like kids; I just didn't think it would happen so soon.

John almost fell over when I got pregnant the first month of our marriage. When we had Cody I immediately knew our lives wouldn't be complete without one more child. We were both approaching forty, so I figured it was now or never. Cody wasn't even five months old when I became pregnant with Jenny, and I didn't go back to work after my maternity leave. I mean, what was the point? A few months later I'd just have to take it over again. I know we were both thrilled at the prospect of being parents again, but John seemed so worried about money. His family had plenty of it, but they squirreled it away for their old age; then they both died young. What was the point?

By the end of our second year of marriage, I was the only breadwinner, while Eileen had her hands full with two really demanding children. On one hand she felt overwhelmed with the children's constant demands, yet she fired nanny who, in her opinion, did not share a similar philosophical view with regard to childcare. Eileen did a great job with them, but as soon as she saw me pull my car into the driveway, she nearly tore the door open to give them to me. Look, I love my kids, but I have a really stressful job, and my idea of coming home wasn't to play Mr. Mom. There were plenty of days in the first five years when Eileen accused me of not wanting the kids. She was wrong. I loved those kids, but I wasn't a real hands-on kind of father. My father wasn't either. He'd look up from the newspaper when I came home from school, say hello, then pull the paper back over his face. I wouldn't see him again until dinner, and even then, he and Mom talked while I sat there quietly. There was no real interaction with my parents. That's they way I was raised, and that's the way it was in most of my friends' houses, too. Eileen came from a much different kind of family.

My mom spent every waking hour with us kids. She didn't have to work, so she always thought up something fun for me and my sisters to do while my dad worked. Either we'd play dress-up with her best clothes and shoes, covering our faces with her makeup, or we'd take a walk and make it an adventure complete with a picnic basket filled with our favorite foods. When Dad came home each night, he'd swoop us up in his arms and want to know all about our day . . . the details, every single one of them. On Saturdays and Sundays he'd join in on the fun, taking us to the lake or to the bowling alley, not bringing us back home until it was way past dark. That's the kind of father I hoped John would be, but he wasn't cut out for playing; he was always worried about work.

I hated to see Eileen have to go back to work. She couldn't get her old job back, things had moved on without her being in the job force for ten years, but she landed a position in an accounting firm, which she seemed to like. I hoped the money I was making would be enough, but I was never able to put anything away after paying the bills. I blamed that on Eileen, and how irresponsible she was with a dollar. I hoped when she realized how hard she had to work for every dime she would be more careful not to buy those kids everything they wanted.

When Cody and Jenny started school, I had to go back to work; things had gotten financially rough, and even with John having a good job, raising the kids cost a lot more than I thought. Of course, I always bought them everything they wanted. Whether it was ice cream or toys, or whatever, if they cried for it, they got it. I just wanted to make sure that when they looked back on their childhood they remembered it being great, just like I remembered mine. I didn't care how much money I spent as long as I was making them happy memories.

Jenny and Cody were completely spoiled by the time they reached middle school. No matter what they wanted, Eileen gave it to them, and what did she get back? Rotten behavior, that's what. Not a thank you, not a kind word; it was like they thought she lived to serve them. They didn't treat me that way, I can tell you that. They knew I'd send them to their rooms, or worse, if they pulled that crap with me. There were days I actually felt a little like I didn't really like them. I mean, of course I loved them, I loved them more than anything else in the world, but I didn't like the way they acted like brats so much of the time. Like this one time, we all went out to a pizza joint. By the time we ordered the damn dinner we had been there an hour. Eileen and I would have eaten the pizza any way it came, but those kids fought over what toppings they wanted, who would sit next to whom, whose chair was wobbly, who didn't get a fork, who didn't like their soda . . . it was a nightmare! And it was a nightmare for the poor waitress, too. She looked at me as if to say, "How could you let your family turn out like this?"

John seemed to be so resentful of the kids when they hit puberty, it was really challenging at home. I thought he should have overlooked their attitudes instead of punishing them every single time they yelled at him. I knew they hated him for it, too. I just said,

"Give them a break, John, they're just kids" and he would go into a rampage, telling the kids they had to go to their rooms for the rest of the night. When John went into his room to read, I snuck them back out into the family room to watch television. It just made me feel so bad for them, having to stay in their rooms without anything to do. They talked badly to me, too, but I just ignored it. I thought it better to ignore their comments than to make a big commotion over it and upset the whole house. I thought that if John kept this up, his kids weren't going to like him very much.

Things went from bad to worse in a relatively short time. Cody was fourteen and thought he knew everything. When I talked to him he stood there glaring at me. He didn't dare talk back; he knew better than that. He knew he'd get something to talk about, all right. But his look said it all. The disrespect he showed Eileen was off the charts, and she did nothing about it. If I heard him, I stepped in, but I wasn't home that much since I had to extend my hours or lose my job to someone who was willing to work late into the evening hours. I couldn't afford to be replaced, so my work week was about fifty hours. Eileen put in almost forty. She felt so guilty that she wasn't home to pamper them when they got home from school that she would put them into the car at least three or four nights a week, buy them fast food, and take them to a movie. On a school night, a movie!

Jenny wasn't too bad, except when she got her period. She thought I didn't know, but Cody ran all over the house announcing it, like he was making a television commercial. I'm not deaf! This would send Jenny into a spin and they fought until someone gave up. I was afraid they were going to hurt each other. They weren't little kids anymore.

When the school called to tell me that Cody was caught skipping class, the first thing I thought of was, how was I going to keep this from John. I just knew he would get all bent out of shape, so I went to school and signed Cody up for after-school suspension, and then I arranged for another mother to pick him up and drive him home on the four nights he had to stay late. It all worked out fine, and John never knew a thing. Cody said he wouldn't do it anymore, so I just figured all's well that ends well.

When Jenny and Cody brought home their report cards I thought I would go through the roof. Neither of them was perfect, but they used to get B's or better. Cody had all D's or insufficient classroom participation, and Jenny got all C's. She said she had a lot to worry about, but I thought her problem was the kid down the street who wanted to be her boyfriend. He was three years older than her, and out of school. I didn't think he had even graduated high school! I told her she better stop worrying about boys and start worrying about her grades unless she wanted to spend her entire summer inside a classroom. As far as Cody was concerned, I made an appointment to see his teachers and get to the bottom of this. For the time being, they were both on restrictions until their grades improved.

John told me he was meeting with Cody's teachers. I tried calling them to tell them not to reveal that Cody had been cutting classes, but they didn't call me back. I didn't know who I could get to cover for me, but no matter what, I couldn't let John know that I had let Cody off the hook. At that point I was more worried about Jenny. She had her head screwed on wrong with this no-good bum down the street; all she could think about was how "hot" he was, which is what worried me. She was nearly sixteen, and almost driving. There was no way I could stop her if she wanted to have sex. I asked her, and she told me she wouldn't, but she did say, as long as we were on the subject, she wanted me to get her birth control pills because she had such bad cramps each month. She said it helped her friends, and why should she have to suffer? I said I'd think about it, but she said if I didn't do it she'd have sex just to punish me, and then we'd see who made the wrong decision. I didn't want to be the reason she was going to have sex, so I made the appointment with my gynecologist for the following week. I told her not to tell her father. She looked at me like I had two heads. Then she said, "As if either one of us tells him anything!"

I got the shock of my life when I sat down with Cody's teachers. They said Cody had cut school for days on end, and before I had recovered from that shock they laid another one on me. Apparently, Eileen knew all about it and set up detention hall as his punishment, without consulting me! I felt like I was losing control of this family; I didn't even recognize my wife anymore. The woman I trusted turned out to be a conspiring liar! My son made a habit of skipping school, and my daughter fell in love with a guy going nowhere fast! I didn't know if I could ever trust Eileen again.

John wasn't as mad as I thought he would be; at least he wasn't screaming. He just looked so hurt, but what was I supposed to do, hang my kid out to dry? These were the best years of our son's life; I didn't want him to spend them in restriction because he didn't do the right things. Anyway, when Jenny got her birth control pills that was one thing off my mind. I got her a special case for them so that no one had to know what they were if they came across them. I was just so tired of all the secrets. I felt like John and I were drifting apart because of the children.

I thought long and hard before I decided to take back the reins of my family. While Eileen and the kids were at the mall one Saturday, I went through every single drawer, every cabinet, every shoe box and storage tub looking for . . . I didn't know *what*. I turned mattresses upside down, pulled boxes out of closets, and got on my hands and knees to search underneath beds. I found the reason Cody was skipping school and had such a lax attitude over the past year about school. I found two small bags of marijuana, a pipe and some rolling paper. I also found stashes of money and papers with phone numbers and names and numbers of what looked like drug orders. In my daughter's room I found birth control pills, naked pictures of her and her boyfriend taken by a third party, and penicillin with a doctor's instructions about how her boyfriend was to take the antibiotic as well, since they were passing an STD back and forth. I also found lacy thong panties and sexy lingerie. I didn't know how much of this my wife knew, but if I found out that she knew about all of it and had kept it from me, I wouldn't be able to stay married to her.

When I came back from the mall, the house had been turned upside down. At first I thought there had been a robbery, but then I realized that John had gathered what he called "evidence" and placed it all in a pile for us to see. He called us into the kitchen and sat us down. There was absolutely no color in either Jenny's or Cody's faces. I thought I was going to have a heart attack. I never knew about the pot, although I have to admit I did suspect it once when I saw Cody's eyes all glassy and weird. I didn't ask about it because I didn't really want to know. I also never knew about Jenny having sex, after she promised she wouldn't! I told John I took her to the doctor to get birth control pills, but it was for her periods. He said I was the dumbest person he'd ever met. When he pulled out the pictures of Jenny and the guy down the street, both naked and engaged in a sex act, I thought I was going to throw up! My little girl, a tramp! That's all I could think of.

I was relieved to see that Eileen didn't know much more than I did, with the exception of the birth control pills. But when these two kids started yelling about their right to privacy and that I had committed an infraction by snooping in their stuff, I almost came unglued. Cody said he could do anything he wanted since his eighteenth birthday was only a few months away, and Jenny said we couldn't stop her from seeing her boyfriend and we had better not try.

I knew things had finally gotten so bad that I couldn't take up for my kids anymore. I guess the money I was always slipping to Cody hadn't gone to school supplies after all, but rather to his drug habit. And Jenny flat out lied to me about those birth control pills. She'd been having sex all that time, and what's worse, I think she'd been having it under my roof! John had told me not to allow her to have her friends over to the house while I was at work, but she seemed so bored to be home alone that I had given in. I just never thought she would bring him *into the house. Now I found that she had contracted a sexually transmitted disease. When I asked how she was able to get an examination and treatment without my permission, she said that HIPPA* (Healthcare Information Portability and Accounting Act) *insured her right to privacy. Imagine, my child, only seventeen years old, was allowed to hide from me the fact that she had a sexually transmitted disease!*

I finally did what I should have done years ago. I confiscated everything that gave my children freedom, including their automobiles, their Internet access, their MySpace accounts, and their money. I told them that when I came to my senses and felt calmer I would call a family meeting to get things back on track. Until then, they were both grounded without access to their friends, their cars, or their computers. They were to check in with me when they got home from school, and again every hour, and they were to call from the house phone so I could track their call with caller I.D. Both children went to their rooms in shock, crying and carrying on, but I didn't care if they cried until the cows came home. As far as I was concerned, the party was over.

It felt as though I was living in a nightmare, like I had lost complete control of my children and my life. I couldn't believe they would do that to me, and yet they did. Me, the one who covered for them and took them everywhere . . . me, the one who gave up every material need I had to make them happy. The craziest things kept going through my head – something my grandmother used to tell me when I was little, a fable she called it, about a frog and a scorpion. It went something like this:

A scorpion needed to get to the other side of a pond, but since he could not swim he asked a frog if he could ride on his back. The frog said he wouldn't take the scorpion to the other side because he was afraid of being stung to death. The scorpion said, as honestly as he could, "Why would I sting you? If I did that, we would both drown." That made a lot of sense to the frog, who finally agreed to give the scorpion a ride on his back across the pond.

Just when they reached the deepest part, in the very center of the pond, the scorpion stung the frog.

"Why would you do such a thing?" the frog asked. "Now we will both die."

The scorpion, as unhappy with his imminent death as the frog was, said, "I don't know. I guess it's just my nature."

It took me two days, but I finally put together a plan which would get the family back on track. On the undercover side of things, and I wasn't proud to admit this, I installed a burglar alarm on all the windows and doors of the house, and hidden cameras throughout the inside and around the outside. It was more money than I could afford, but I took out a loan . . . that's how serious I was about knowing every coming and going of this family. Then, I sat each person down and told them the new rules in no uncertain terms. We made a behavior chart with consequences that were going to be upheld by me. I instructed Eileen that until she could resolve her own part in this, I wouldn't be able to trust her judgment with rules. Then I took away every privilege they had, including their cars. I arranged transportation to and from school with a neighbor, who I agreed to pay. They were allowed their cell phones, to be used only in case of emergencies, and I signed up for a plan with a company that regulated the numbers they were allowed to call, decided by me; every other number was blocked. Last, I took away all of their money. Anything they needed would be purchased by me, when I got to it, and not before. I didn't know how long these new rules would need to remain in effect but they would stay in place until I felt that Cody and Jenny had begun to earn my trust. I thought it could be quite a while.

I was actually relieved that John took the burden of the kids on his shoulders. In hindsight, I know I helped the children sabotage their father's relationship with them, and really was an accessory to their bad behavior, even though it was unintentional. I thought his punishments were pretty harsh, but I'll say one thing, it certainly got their attention. When he came home from work and we were in the house, he would put the alarm on with a special code on the keypad in our bedroom. No one could get in or out without his knowledge, and, I have to say, I slept better without the worry of the unknown.

* * *

Hi, we're the kids, Cody and Jenny. You haven't heard the story from our side yet, so here goes. Whatever you think you know, it was ten times worse. Both of us had gotten into trouble that could actually have endangered our lives, Cody with drug people, and me with my boyfriend. He was pretty abusive, and liked to push me around. He was mean, too, but after a while I didn't think I could do better, because he told me I couldn't. Once the money ran out, he ran out. It took me a few months to rebalance, but my life got so much better after he left. Cody and I are closer now than ever before. We had to be. We were the only people we were allowed to hang out with for almost six months, until Mom and Dad gave us freedom, a little at a time. They did us a big favor, and we will be eternally grateful. Both of us went to college, and Cody went on to medical school. As for me, I met a man who thinks I'm wonderful and has asked me to marry him. Because Mom no longer works, I am expected to pitch in for the wedding expenses, which I think is really fair, especially after how much my parents have sacrificed for me over the years. As for Dad, he's one year from retirement, and he and Mom have been looking at travel magazines, planning the second half of their lives. Both Cody and I only hope we can take these lessons and teach them to our children some day. It's not about the money or the freedom. It's not about the material possessions or the friends you thought were so important, who mean nothing to you now. It's about unconditional love that bonds a family together, through the worst of times and the best of times. Our parents' love and dedication have given us the best of times.

Epilogue

The struggle of adolescence has become a scrapbook of memories: your child's name in a program for the second grade Christmas pageant; report cards showing perfect attendance; chaperoning the sixth-grade school trip; a request from the dean for a parent/teacher meeting; crumpled notes from a diary that explained everything; a prom date who backed out just two days before the big night; the dented fender on the brand new car. How you have come to the end of your child's teenage years with your wits still about you is nothing short of a miracle. But now, as you stand staring at the footlockers and duffle bags that line the front hallway, all the arguing, the late nights of missed curfews and the uncompleted chores seem a million years away from what is about to occur.

The flurry of activity is about to be quieted, and your teenager is about to move on to college. The worry over their giving up their future to run away with a steady girlfriend or boyfriend when they were only fifteen seems trivial now, compared to the emptiness that has already permeated the house. As you catch a last glimpse of their boundless energy you hope that every fact you have ever known, every incident you can ever remember, every situation you have ever experienced has been passed along and will serve as a guideline when you are not there, by their side, to do the laundry, cook the dinner, pack lunches, and look in on them while they sleep. You hope they will be happy, make good grades, meet new friends, and follow the right path. Most of all, you hope they know how very much you love them.

Resources and Help for Parents

By now you probably realize that parenting a teenager is second in confusion to actually being a teenager; both have their categories of worries and concerns, and successful mastery of these challenges is in direct proportion to the understanding, approach, and resolution of specific issues and problems as they arise. It is often not enough to use love alone as the criteria by which to parent an adolescent, because emotional attachment often clouds the issues at hand, and the job of parenting cannot always be done without a strong support system, be that a spouse or former spouse, friends, family, clergy, and public and private resources. There are a multitude of resources available to assist both you and your son or daughter as they venture down the path toward emotional maturity.

Immediate Assistance

In a medical emergency or emotional crisis, you should never hesitate to call for help or go directly to your nearest hospital emergency room. Even if your teenager tells you that "it's nothing," if your gut feeling tells you that something doesn't look or feel right, please do the right thing, which is to enlist the opinion of a professional.

In a non-emergency, there are a multitude of resources available at the other end of your telephone. We have included below a thorough list for your information and peace of mind. These agencies and their staff are there specifically to answer your questions and point you in the right direction. Please do not underestimate their value.

THE LIST	
24-hour Hotline: Emergency or Drug overdose	911
Abandoned Infant Hotline	1-866-505-7233
Adolescent Resources Parent Hotline	1-800-400-0900
Alcohol and Other Drug Services	1-800-565-7450
Alcohol and Substance Abuse Services	1-800-553-5790
Association of Anorexia Nervosa and Associated Eating Disorders (ANAD)	1-800-762-7402
Banking: Consumer Info and Complaints	1-877-226-5697
Child Protective Services	1-800-565-4304
Crime Stoppers	1-800-255-1301
Daycare Complaint Hotline	1-800-732-5207
Emergency Shelter for Teens:	
The Coffee House Shelter	1-800-544-3299 or 1-800-546-3432
The Drop Inn	1-800-568-4415
Gambling Information	1-800-437-1611
HIV Information and Testing	1-800-565-4620
HIV Nightline 5 P.M. – 5 A.M. daily	1-800-273-2437
Missing and Exploited Children	1-800-FIND-KID
National Youth Crisis Hotline	1-800-448-4663
Positive Images (Gay & Lesbian)	1-800-579-4947
Pregnancy Counseling Center	1-800-575-9000
Psychiatric Emergency Services	1-800-746-8181
QUEST (Intensive out-patient program for eating disorders)	1-800-284-2162
Rape Hotline	1-800-545-7273
Social Advocates for Youth Emergency	1-800-544-3299
United Against Sexual Assault	1-800-545-7270
YWCA Domestic Violence Hotline	1-800-546-1234

Support Teams for Parents

A multitude of resources are available to parents, beginning with the support of friends who are parenting teens of their own. Comparing notes makes your problems seem less isolated to your family and offers a sounding board to vent your concerns. That said, if you find that after you have compared notes your teenager's behavior doesn't seem to fall within the norms, you really should consult professional guidance, enlisting a licensed clinical psychologist or licensed clinical social worker to evaluate and, if necessary, treat your child.

Parenting coaches are available in some areas of the country and can be found by searching on the Internet. Such coaches are not licensed to diagnose and treat disorders but can offer support and guidance about normal, but frustrating, problems for which you need some objective assistance. Parenting coaches may be available for a lecture series that is open to the general public, or may be retained for private sessions at your home. The price of such services is less than that of a psychologist, but the advice offered will generally focus more on resistant behavior, or passing defiance. For something more severe, such as "oppositional defiant disorder," a licensed professional is the person to call. Depending on your healthcare plan, a psychologist or psychiatrist may be covered by your insurance. Call ahead about the office policy with regard to insurance, and then call your insurance agent to speak with a representative who can quote coverage over the telephone prior to your visit.

Parenting Chats

If you like the ease and accessibility of the Internet, there are parenting groups and chat lines pertaining to parenting teenagers on the Web; however, these groups often come and go and, although helpful, should be used only as an adjunct to other sources of information. Many of the contributors in these groups are parents struggling to find answers and are not equipped to give accurate advice.

Books to Help You Parent

Finally, there are books available both in the library and on bookstore shelves that address the subjects of teenagers, drugs and alcohol, and making and enforcing boundaries. Not every book will fit in with your philosophy of parenting, but any book you choose should offer direct, well-thought-out plans for dealing with your child's challenges, as well as advice that does not waiver or try to cover both sides of the fence. Otherwise, you will have gained nothing and added to already mounting confusion. You have only a small window of opportunity within which to impart everything you need your teenagers to know before they march off into the world independently; do not cloud that window with indecision and confusion. See the Bibliography that follows for our suggestions of parenting books.

Conclusion

The most important thing to remember is this: Your teenager needs you. He or she needs your wisdom, your experience, your patience, your kindness and your love. They also need you to be strong enough to discipline them with consequences that will leave a lasting impression and teach a lesson. Without all of these ingredients, your adolescent will be ill-prepared to face the world as an emotionally happy, independent and valuable member of society. The lessons you teach today will shape the person they will become tomorrow. Make every lesson count.

Bibliography

Baksh, Nadir, Psy.D., and Laurie Murphy, Ph.D. *In The Best Interest of the Child: A Manual For Divorcing Parents*. Prescott, Arizona: Hohm Press, 2007.

Borowitz, Susan. *When We're in Public Pretend You Don't Know Me*. New York: Warner Books, 2003.

Fleming, Don, Ph.D. *How to Stop the Battle with Your Teenager*. New York: Simon and Shuster, 1993.

Foster, Clive, M.D. and Jim Fay. *Parenting Teens with Love and Logic*. Pinon Press, 1992, 2006.

Freud, Sigmund, *The Interpretation of Dreams*. New York: Barnes and Noble Classics, 2005.

Giannetti, Charlene and Margaret Sagarese. *The Roller Coaster Years*. New York: Broadway Books, 1997.

Pasick, Patricia, Ph.D. *Almost Grown*. New York: W.W. Norton and Co., 1998.

Phelan, Thomas, Ph.D. *Surviving Your Adolescents*. Glen Ellyn, Illinois: Parentmagic Inc., 1998.

Riera, Michael, Ph.D. *Stay Connected to Your Teenager*. Cambridge, Massachusetts: Da Capo Books, 2003.

Strauch, Barbara. *The Primal Teen*. New York: Anchor Books, 2003.

Walsh, David, Ph.D. *Why Do They Act That Way?* New York: Free Press, 2004.

Walsh, David, Ph.D. *No – Why Kids of All Ages Need to Hear It and Ways Parents Can Say It*. New York: Free Press, 2007.

Index

A

absentmindedness, 56–57
abuse, 139. *See also* sexual abuse
academic help, 131–32
academic needs and performance,
    129–30, 148
adult supervision, 87
agriculture, 24–25
alcohol, 104–5. *See also* drug use
angry outbursts, 20–22
animals, violence to, 139
anorexia nervosa, 37–38, 126
anxiety, teen, 33–34, 36–39, 46, 140–41.
    See also specific topics
apologizing, 19–21
Asperger's syndrome, 42

B

babysitting, 29
bedtime designations, 109–11
behavior and consequences, 137–38. *See
    also* consequences; *specific topics*
behavioral chart, 51–55, 62
books on parenting, 159
boundaries/boundary setting, 13–15,
    106
    around money, 117–20
    bedtime and curfew, 109–12
    and both parents, 107
    study, 112–13
brain, teenage, 28–31
bulimia, 37–38, 126
bullying, 41, 43. *See also* misfits

C

cell phone, owning a, 122
chat rooms, Internet, 101–3

child abuse, 139. *See also* sexual abuse
chores, 23–25
clothing, 90–91
college admissions information, 134–36
college prep, 132–34
communication, 52–53
computer matters, privacy in, 101–3
consequences, 49–52, 58
consistency, 65–66
    duration, 58–59
    fairness, 55
    healthy fear of, 63–64
    vs. punishment, 51
    seriousness, 58
    staying realistic/balanced in
        deciding on, 61–63
    taking away their stuff, 61–63
    "the look," 64–65
cosmetic surgery, 125
courage, 128
credit card use, 94
curfews, 109–12
"cutting," 37–39

D

dating, 113–15
debates, 16–18
decision making, 29–31. *See also*
    responsibilities
delinquency, 137–40
democracy, 18–19
depression, 36–40, 140–41
discipline. *See* consequences
disrespect, 13–15, 20–22, 48–50
    defined, 48–49
doctors, 124–26
dress, 90–91

driving a car, 120–22
drug use, 77, 81, 99. *See also* steroid use
    testing for, 99, 105–6, 127–28
drugs
    privacy and, 104–6

E
eating disorders, 37, 126
emotional health, 128. *See also specific topics*
exploitation, 23–25
extracurricular activities, 95

F
failure, admitting, 19–21
fairness. *See under* consequences
fashion, 90–91
fear. *See also* anxiety
    of parents, healthy, 63–64
    related to privacy, 103–4
    of your teenager, 137–38
fires, 138–39
forgetfulness, 56–57
friendship with children, 31–32

G
grades, 130, 148
guilt, 53
gynecological checkups, 124

H
health, 123–24. *See also* illness; sickness
hierarchy, importance of, 18–19
homeschooling, 46–47
honesty. *See* lying
hotlines, 157

I
illness, 123–24. *See also* sickness
In the Best Interests of the Child: A Manual for Divorcing Parents (Baksh and Murphy), 106

Internet, 101–3
    pornography on, 101–2, 140

J
juvenile delinquency, 137–40

L
labtop computers, 102
"lazy" *vs.* tired, 112
leaders and followers, learning to be good, 87–89
"lights out" rule, 109–11
limit setting. *See* boundaries/boundary setting; consequences
love
    expressing/demonstrating, 8–10
    the idea and reality of, 8–10
    unconditional, 22
lying, 67–69, 74–75
    degrees of, 70–71

M
manipulation, 72–73, 83–84
    high-stakes, 77–83
    identifying, 84–86
    rewards for sickness, 76–77
materialism, 27
mental health, 128. *See also specific topics*
misfits, dangerous, 40–43
    information and protection, 43–47
missing children, 97
mistakes, admitting, 19–21
money, 27, 92–93
    boundaries around, 117–20
mononucleosis, 123

O
organization, 122

P
"parental rejection," 20–22

parenting
  the business of, 5–7
  emotional *vs.* business aspects, 5
parenting chats, 158–59
parents
  becoming our, 10–11
  befriending children, 31–32
  resources and help for, 156–59
  immediate assistance, 156–57
  on trial, 3–5
peer pressures, 34
perfection, 19
physical appearance, 124–27
plastic surgery, 125
pornography, 140
  Internet, 101–2, 140
power, 19
predators, Internet, 101–3
pregnancy, 30
privacy, 98–100, 151
  in computer matters, 101–3
  drugs and, 104–6
  facing your fears related to, 103–4
psychiatric treatment, 137, 141
punishment. *See* consequences

R
reminders, 55–58
"rescuing" children, 12
resource officers, 43
respect, 13–15, 48–50. *See also*
  disrespect
responsibilities, 23–25
  giving teenagers, 12, 23–24, 28–29
  and the teenage brain, 28–31
rewards, 59
rules, 18–19, 28, 56–57

S
safety, 94–97. *See also under* shopping
  malls
scholarships, 133, 135

self-inflicted injury/self-mutilation, 37–39
sex and the teenager, 115–17, 148–51
sexual abuse, 39, 102–3, 139
shopping malls
  safety at, 88–92
  whose money they spend at, 92–94
sickness, rewards for, 76–77
sleep, 109, 112
social outcasts. *See* misfits
socialization, 26. *See also specific topics*
  college prep and, 95
  problems related to, 100. *See also*
    specific problems
supporting, 96–97
space, giving teenagers, 12
staph infections, 123–24
steroid use, 127
stimulation overload, 35–36, 40
suicide, 141–42
supervision, adult, 87
support teams for parents, 158

T
team approach, xi–xii
teasing, 44–45. *See also* misfits
teenagers. *See also specific topics*
  comparing them with their friends
    or siblings, 20–21
  knowing where they are, 97
  "passing inspection" each time they
    leave house, 90–91
  putting parents on trial, 3–5
television, 110
theft, 138
time pressures, 34–35
times, changing, 26–28
tracking, 130
truancy, 139–40

V
violence. *See also* abuse
  to animals, 139

Other Titles of Interest from Hohm Press

IN THE BEST INTEREST OF THE CHILD
A Manual for Divorcing Parents
by Nadir Baksh, Psy.D. and Laurie Murphy, R.N., Ph.D.

This book will help parents save their children unnecessary anguish throughout the divorce process. Written by a licensed clinical psychologist, and a nurse and counselor, the authors have a private practice with families and also work as court-appointed evaluators in child-custody disputes.

Their advice and direction is eminently practical – detailing what adults can expect from a custody battle; what they will encounter in themselves and in their children (emotionally, physically, mentally) during divorce; advising how parents can make sense out of children's questions; offering guidance in making decisions for themselves and their kids; and explaining the ultimate importance of putting the child's needs first.

Paper, 144 pages, 6 x 9 inches, $16.95   ISBN: 978-1-890772-73-4

CONSCIOUS PARENTING
by Lee Lozowick

Any individual who cares for children needs to attend to the essential message of this book: that the first two years are the most crucial time in a child's education and development, and that children learn to be healthy and "whole" by living with healthy, whole adults.

Offers practical guidance and help for anyone who wishes to bring greater consciousness to every aspect of childraising, including: * conception, pregnancy and birth * emotional development * language usage * role modeling: the mother's role, the father's role * the exposure to various influences * establishing workable boundaries * the choices we make on behalf on our children's education ... and much more. [**Available at a reduced price as publisher's seconds only**]

Paper, 378 pages, formerly $17.95.   ISBN: 978-0-934252-67-6

166

STAINLESS HEART
The Wisdom of Remorse
by Clelia Vahni

Anyone who has ever felt guilt will find both comfort and direction in this clearly written and compassionate book. The "stainless heart" is Clelia Vahni's description of the pure, essential nature of the human being. This heart, however, is rarely touched. One reason for this impasse, the author states, is that we have built walls around the heart, out of shame; or have held ourselves apart so we don't get hurt anymore (or hurt others) because we are afraid of the pain that guilt carries. Guilt is different from genuine remorse, the author argues. Guilt destroys us, while true remorse is the entry into truth, to a clear vision of life "as it is," and thus to a transformed relationship to ourselves and others. "The voice of remorse," she writes, "is a call from our stainless heart, challenging us to make the effort necessary to live by its wisdom."

Paper, 160 pages, $12.95   ISBN: 978-1-890772-40-6

THE SHADOW ON THE PATH
Clearing the Psychological Blocks to Spiritual Development
by VJ Fedorschak
Foreword by Claudio Naranjo, M.D.

Tracing the development of the human psychological shadow from Freud to the present, this readable analysis presents five contemporary approaches to spiritual psychotherapy for those who find themselves needing help on the spiritual path. Offers insight into the phenomenon of denial and projection.

Topics include: the shadow in the Work; notable therapists; the principles of inner spiritual development in the major world religions; examples of the disowned shadow in contemporary religious movements; and case studies of clients in spiritual groups who have worked with their shadow issues.

Paper, 300 pages, $17.95   ISBN: 978-0-934252-81-2

To Order: 800-381-2700, or visit our website, www.hohmpress.com

THE JUMP INTO LIFE
Moving Beyond Fear
by Arnaud Desjardins
Foreword by Richard Moss, M.D.

"Say *Yes* to life," the author continually invites in this welcome guidebook to the spiritual path. For anyone who has ever felt oppressed by the life-negative seriousness of religion, this book is a timely antidote. In language that translates the complex to the obvious, Desjardins applies his simple teaching of happiness and gratitude to a broad range of weighty topics, including: sexuality and intimate relationships, structuring an "inner life," the relief of suffering, and overcoming fear.

Paper, 278 pages, $12.95   ISBN: 978-0-934252-42-3

THE ACTIVE CREATIVE CHILD
Parenting in Perpetual Motion
by Stephanie Vlahov

Active/creative children are often misunderstood by the medical community, by schools, and by their own parents. Their energy is astounding; their inquisitiveness is boundless. Channeling that energy is not only helpful, but necessary. Supporting that inquisitiveness is essential! This book provides specific hints for coping, for establishing realistic boundaries, and for avoiding labels and easy judgments where any child is concerned. Written in a simple, journalistic style, the author draws from her experience with her two active/creative sons, and those of others, to present a handbook of encouragement and genuine help.

Paper, 105 pages, $ 9.95   ISBN: 978-1-890772-47-5

To Order: 800-381-2700, or visit our website, www.hohmpress.com

TO TOUCH IS TO LIVE
The Need for Genuine Affection in an Impersonal World
by Mariana Caplan
Foreword by Ashley Montagu

The vastly impersonal nature of contemporary culture, supported by massive child abuse and neglect, and reinforced by growing techno-fascination are robbing us of our humanity. The author takes issue with the trends of the day that are mostly overlooked as being "progressive" or harmless, showing how these trends are actually undermining genuine affection and love. This uncompromising and inspiring work offers positive solutions for countering the effects of the growing depersonalization of our times.

"An important book that brings to the forefront the fundamentals of a healthy world. We must all touch more." – Patch Adams, M.D.

Paper, 272 pages, $19.95   ISBN: 978-1-890772-24-6

WHEN SONS AND DAUGHTERS CHOOSE
ALTERNATIVE LIFESTYLES
by Mariana Caplan

A guidebook for families in building workable relationships based on trust and mutual respect, despite the fears and concerns brought on by differences in lifestyle. Practical advice on what to do when sons and daughters (brothers, sisters, grandchildren ...) join communes, go to gurus, follow rock bands around the country, marry outside their race or within their own gender, or embrace a religious belief that is alien to that of parents and family.

"Recommended for all public libraries."—*Library Journal.*

Paper, 264 pages, $14.95   ISBN: 978-0-934252-69-0

To Order: 800-381-2700, or visit our website, www.hohmpress.com

PARENTING, A SACRED TASK
10 Basics of Conscious Childraising
by Karuna Fedorschak

Moving beyond our own self-centered focus and into the realm of generosity and expansive love is the core of spiritual practice. This book can help us to make that move. It highlights 10 basic elements that every parent can use to meet the everyday demands of childraising. Turning that natural duty into a sacred task is what this book is about. Topics include: love, attention, boundaries, food, touch, help and humor.

"There is no more rigorous path to spiritual development than that of being a parent. Thank you to Karuna Fedorschak for reminding us that parenting is a sacred task." – Peggy O'Mara, Editor and Publisher, *Mothering Magazine*.

Paper, 158 pages, $12.95   ISBN: 978-1-890772-30-7

ROSIE, THE SHOPPING-CART LADY
by Chia Martin
Illustrations by Jewel Hernandez

This children's picture book tells what happens when a sensitive little boy confronts the hard reality of a disheveled old woman who wanders the city streets collecting trash or treasures in her shopping cart. It addresses neither the global questions of injustice nor a specific solution to the massive problem of homelessness in the U.S. today. Rather, easy-rhyming text and colorful illustrations highlight a story designed to inspire questions and conversation about this important subject.

"This heartwarming story is a reminder of the need for each of us to become involved in our communities. It is never too early to learn the message contained in *Rosie*. – Elaine L. Chao, President and CEO, United Way of America

Hardcover, 32 pages; 16 full-color illustrations, $15.95
ISBN: 978-0-934252-51-5

To Order: 800-381-2700, or visit our website, www.hohmpress.com

THE WAY OF FAILURE
Winning Through Losing
by Mariana Caplan

This straight-talking and strongly inspirational book looks failure directly in the face, unmasking it for what it really is. Mariana Caplan tells us to how to meet failure on its own field, how to learn its twists and turns, as well as its illusions and realities. Only then, she advises, is one equipped to engage failure as a means of ultimate "winning," and in a way that far exceeds our culturally-defined visions of success.

Paper, 144 pages, $14.95   ISBN: 978-1-890772-10-9

THE WOMAN AWAKE
Feminine Wisdom for Spiritual Life
by Regina Sara Ryan

Through the stories and insights of great women of spirit whom the author has met or been guided by in her own journey, this book highlights many faces of the Divine Feminine: the silence, the solitude, the service, the power, the compassion, the art, the darkness, the sexuality. Read about: the Sufi poetess Rabia (8th century) and contemporary Sufi master Irina Tweedie; Christian saints Hildegard of Bingen, Mechtild of Magdeburg and Hadewijch of Brabant; the Beguines of medieval Europe; author Kathryn Hulme (*The Nun's Story*) who worked with Gurdjieff; German healer and mystic Dina Rees, Zen roshi Joan Halifax ... and many others.

Paper, 35 b&w photos, 520 pages, $19.95   ISBN: 978-0-934252-79-9

To Order: 800-381-2700, or visit our website, www.hohmpress.com

KISHIDO
The Way of the Western Warrior
by Peter Hobart

The code of the samurai and the path of the knight-warrior – traditions from opposite sides of the globe – find a common ground in *Kishido: The Way of the Western Warrior*. In fifty short essays, Peter Hobart presents the wisdom, philosophy and teachings of the mysterious Master who first united the noble houses of East and West. Kishido prioritizes the ideals of duty, ethics, courtesy and chivalry, from whatever source they derive. This cross-cultural approach represents a return to time-honored principles from many traditions, and allows the modern reader from virtually any background to find the master within.

Paper, 130 pages; $12.95   ISBN: 978-1-890772-31-4

YOU HAVE THE RIGHT TO REMAIN SILENT
Bringing Meditation to Life
by Rick Lewis

With sparkling clarity and humor, Rick Lewis explains exactly what meditation can offer to those who are ready to establish an island of sanity in the midst of an active life. This book is a comprehensive look at everything a beginner would need to start a meditation practice, including how to befriend an overactive mind and how to bring the fruits of meditation into all aspects of daily life. Experienced meditators will also find refreshing perspectives to both nourish and refine their practice.

Paper, 201 pages, $14.95   ISBN: 978-1-890772-23-9

To Order: 800-381-2700, or visit our website, www.hohmpress.com

YOGA FROM THE INSIDE OUT
Making Peace with Your Body through Yoga
by Christina Sell

This book is about yoga and body image. It is about the journey from various addictions and self-hatred into self-acceptance leading to spiritual practice. It is based in the principles of Anusara Yoga, a style of hatha yoga that integrates physical practice with inner body awareness and a deep connection to the heart. Christina Sell is a certified instructor of Anusara Yoga. In her own life and those of her friends and students, she has seen the devastating effects of the war against the body.

"Christina reminds us that practicing yoga is so much more than just postures and breathing. It is a deeply personal journey back home to ourselves, and it takes us from self-doubt and judgment to self-acceptance and joy." – Judith Hanson Lasater, Ph.D.

Paper, 144 pages, b&w photos, $14.95   ISBN: 978-1-890772-32-1

THE WILL TO HEALTH
Inertia, Change, and Choice
by Robert I. Reynolds, Ph.D., N.D.

The Will to Health is about making the changes that determine our health, and why some people do it while others apparently don't. But it goes further, pointing to how "the will to live" – which the author calls the "will to health" – can be achieved by working through the natural inertia that normally tends to stop us.

In two-dozen fascinating case studies, Dr. Reynolds, a psychoanalyst and naturopathic physician, introduces us to people with chronic illness who have successfully made a life-saving choice. By clarifying their sense of will or purpose, each patient was able to move beyond their ordinary limits of psychology, belief or environment.

Paper, 224 pages, $14.95   ISBN: 978-1-890772-39-0

To Order: 800-381-2700, or visit our website, www.hohmpress.com

About the Authors

Nadir Baksh, Psy.D. is a Licensed Clinical Psychologist specializing in Clinical and Forensic Psychology since 1984. He is a Fellow of the American Association of Integrative Medicine and the American Board of Forensic Examiners, and Diplomate of the American Psychotherapy Association, with over twenty-two years of clinical experience in office practice. Throughout this time, Dr. Baksh has successfully treated hundreds of troubled teens, parents and family members. He is the coauthor of *In the Best Interest of the Child: A Manual for Divorcing Parents.*

Laurie Elizabeth Murphy, R.N., Ph.D. is a registered nurse counselor who works with teenagers and their families. The mother of four grown children, Dr. Murphy's successful practice reflects her belief that the most rebellious of teens want to be loved and praised, and with the proper mix of boundaries and love can break through their own defiance to reach their potential. She is the coauthor of *In the Best Interest of the Child: A Manual for Divorcing Parents.*

Contact Information

Laurie Murphy and Nadir Baksh have an active website. Please visit them at www.InTheBestInterestOfTheChildren.com. Use the *Contact Us* section on the website to send your questions, and they will try to answer as many as possible. They also love comments from readers. Send correspondence to 421 Martin Avenue, Stuart, Florida 34996.